D0226356

Literacy
in Colonial New England

Literacy in
Colonial New England

*An Enquiry into the
Social Context of Literacy in
the Early Modern West*

KENNETH A. LOCKRIDGE

W·W·NORTON & COMPANY · INC·
NEW YORK

WITHDRAWN
LIBRARY
COLLEGE
EMMITSBURG, MARYLAND

Copyright © 1974 by W. W. Norton & Company, Inc.
First Edition

Library of Congress Cataloging in Publication Data
Lockridge, Kenneth A
  Literacy in colonial New England.
  Bibliography: p.
  1. Illiteracy—New England—History. I. Title.
LC152.N57L62   301.44′5   74-2168
ISBN 0-393-05522-1
ISBN 0-393-09263-1 (pbk)

All Rights Reserved
Published simultaneously in Canada
by George J. McLeod Limited, Toronto

Printed in the United States of America

1 2 3 4 5 6 7 8 9 0

This book was designed by Andrea Clark.
The type is Janson and Caslon 540, set by Spartan Typographers.
Printed and bound by Vail-Ballou Press, Inc.

To Hal, Jackie, Debbie, Penny, Chris, Ginny,
Annegret, Jack, Jeanie, Betsy . . .

Preface

THIS study of literacy in colonial New England suggests
that we cannot see more than the faintest origins of modernity in the social context of literacy in this region or perhaps in any part of the early modern West. It remains for
others to confirm or deny this supposition. The scholars
who will finally understand the role of literacy in early
western society, and so grasp the nature of that society, are
the men whose encouragement has made this study possible.
To Roger Schofield and Egil Johansson, sincere thanks and
best wishes for their own efforts. Others who must be mentioned are Frank Craven and Lawrence Stone, mentors in
all my researches. Professor Stone, in conjunction with the
members of the Shelby Cullom Davis seminar, has made the
most constructive criticisms of this manuscript. Kathy Crit-
tenden and Mary Hyde were essential to the data processing
and statistical analysis, though neither is responsible for un-
conscious flights of statistical fancy. Judith Hanson and
Elaine Wethington have been everything from designers and
prosecutors of research to analysts of the data.

Contents

[ix]

Graphs

Literacy
in Colonial New England

I

Literacy in
Colonial New England

·⊹·⊹·

WHILE coding wills for an historical study of charitable behavior in America and in England, I decided to code the
"literacy" of some early Americans, chiefly of persons leaving wills in colonial New England. Persons signing their
wills I took to be literate, as opposed to those who made
only a mark. Presumably this would be most valid for aggregates of signers versus aggregates of markers, but I was
willing to assume that there would be a real difference in
literacy between any given signer and any given marker.

This variable soon became more interesting than charitable behavior. Assuming that signers were more literate
than markers, to what extent does the literacy rate of persons leaving wills approximate the true pattern of literacy
in colonial New England? How widespread was literacy in
seventeenth-century New England? Was literacy expanding, if so, at what rate? What was the "social structure"
of literacy, that is, who was literate and who was not and
how was this changing with time? What difference did it
make to a man to be literate, or to society that literacy
was wide or spreading? Specifically, did literacy ever entail qualitative changes in human attitudes? Why did literacy perform as it did? What were the sources of literacy,

[3]

the sources of any massive increases in literacy, in this region of the American past?

The exercise is bound to be tentative, as it uses a biased sample and an ambiguous measure. Still, signatures on wills suggest a portrait of the level, trend, social structure, attitudinal or qualitative correlates, and causal sources of literacy in colonial New England. The results are surprisingly "traditional." It appears that New England experienced several generations of mass illiteracy before achieving nearly universal male literacy toward the end of the colonial period. The eventual advent of universal male literacy transformed the social structure of literacy by erasing correlations between social status and this basic skill. Yet there is no evidence that literacy ever entailed new attitudes among men, even in the decades when male literacy was spreading rapidly toward universality, and there is positive evidence that the world view of literate New Englanders remained as traditional as that of their illiterate neighbors. Women's literacy improved, but female illiteracy remained quite common and women were always at a distinct disadvantage in obtaining basic education. The reason behind this reluctant revolution may be that in New England a major source of personal literacy, and the source above all of the rise in male literacy, appears to have been the system of public schools established for essentially religious reasons. With increasing social concentration these schools became more readily available, hence more effective in raising male literacy. Their stated motives included neither the displacement of men's attitudes from traditional concerns nor the improvement of the relative status of women. From all the evidence, New England was a Puritan society which achieved its goal of universal male literacy to essentially conservative ends.

These results imply that literacy in the rest of colonial America showed an even less dynamic aspect than in New England. Lacking that intense Protestantism which provided systematic schooling, the other colonies may not have achieved even the eventual rise toward universal male literacy attained in New England. Illiteracy may have remained common among both sexes. The correlation of social status with male literacy may have remained strong. Under such circumstances there is no reason to believe that those who did become literate would have imbibed new attitudes with their literacy. Evidence drawn from eighteenth-century Pennsylvania and Virginia confirms these suspicions. Literacy here was stagnant, albeit on a respectable level, and highly correlated with social status, while literates remained traditional in their attitudinal patterns. This is precisely the pattern of literacy which prevailed in England at the time.

This and wider evidence indicates that the eighteenth-century Atlantic world lacked those powerful forces which today revolutionize the breadth, structure, and very meaning of literacy in developing nations. Protestantism was perhaps the sole force which could rapidly increase literacy to high levels or bring the level of this skill to universality. It was effective chiefly in small societies whose Protestant concern was strong, widespread, and uniform enough to prevail upon the state church or the state itself to provide or compel systematic education. Even there, Protestantism's effects seem to have extended only to the breadth of literacy. New England was such a society, and so was Scotland, where literacy progressed as rapidly, and so was Sweden, where there was an astoundingly rapid spread of literacy among both men and women late in the seventeenth century. Beneath the intense if perhaps limited educational dynamism of Sweden, below the significant achievements of Scotland and New England, the forces at work were real but relatively minor. The force of migration, or of culture (including a more diffuse Protestantism), or of social concentration, or of mere wealth, determined that in the long run colonial America would achieve a slightly higher level of technical literacy than England, and England a higher level than France, and so forth, and that within these nations one generation or locality or person

[5]

would achieve a higher literacy than another. Yet these forces were not such as to raise literacy anywhere rapidly to universality, much less alter its structure or quality, the latter an effect not even Puritanism could achieve. Such forces did not exist in the world we have lost, the world of rural, preindustrial, western society.

While interesting, these tentative conclusions will not be surprising to most students of the past, who have known all along that it was not like the present. The direction of the evidence will, however, be surprising to readers of the current literature on the early history of American education.[1] Readers of this literature have been led to expect that in colonial America the combined forces of the wilderness and of social mobility led everywhere to a dynamic educational ethos. Presumably this ethos was powerful enough to increase literacy until it encompassed nearly all men in the colonies, while intensifying in them certain "liberating" attitudinal transformations. These readers will not expect religion to be the sole source of the only substantial rise in colonial American literacy. They will not anticipate an educational ethos which otherwise could not raise the level of literacy throughout large areas of the eighteenth-century colonies. They will not expect to find a massive minority of men in these areas simply ineligible for the benefits of whatever educational ethos existed in the absence of Puritanism. They will not expect to find in large areas a continuing association of literacy with wealth and high status. They will be surprised to find evidence in New England and elsewhere in America that men who became literate, and so entered the influence of the educational ethos, acquired none of the aspects of the "individualistic, optimistic, and enterprising" personality of modern man. Looking in vain for a precociously modern "American" ethos, these readers may be startled to find instead a world of the past, a world America shared with Europe.

For those who already accept the implications of the data, this monograph will at least announce the beginning of an effort to view American literacy in a comparative historical perspective, and will introduce the difficulties of learning more from early American literacy within this calmer frame.

From Measured to True Literacy

The measure used here is the level of signatures among a sample of persons leaving wills in colonial New England.[2] Do signatures measure literacy? If so, how does the signature literacy of this sample relate to that of the population of New England?

The answer to the first question is "yes." Scholars agree that the level of signatures runs below but closely parallels reading skills and runs above but roughly parallels writing skills. While the absolute level of either literacy skill must remain uncertain, comparisons of the signature levels of various groups yield fairly reliable comparisons of their relative levels of overall literacy. Under this interpretation the most precise *absolute* definition which could be placed on signatures is that they correspond to the actual level of fluent reading.[3]

The issue, then, is whether the signatures of the persons in this sample of New England wills correspond to the signature level in the population.[4] The answer again is "yes," and for an odd reason. People leaving wills were older, richer, and of higher occupational status than the rest of the population. Various biases of old age mitigate against signatures yet the biases of wealth and of occupation work in favor of signatures. The two sets of biases appear to cancel, leaving signatures on wills a fair facsimile of signatures among the population. The conclusion is that signatures on wills approximate the literacy not only of the sample but of the population.

SEVERAL biases resulting from the age of the persons in the sample tended to reduce its level of signatures below the level of the population. None of these biases was powerful,

[7]

even at its maximum, and probably all were declining. But cumulatively they merit consideration.

Feebleness is one example. There is no doubt that some persons who made wills were too weak to sign their names, although they knew how. Yet only a third of the persons in this sample made their wills within three months of probate, so most wills seem to have been made before impending death could palsy a literate hand. In the case of one hundred fully literate ministers, only two made marks on their wills, a small toll for feebleness. The figure for gentlemen was 8%, but illiterate gentlemen were not unknown, so not every mark represents a literate man struck down by feebleness. There are hypothetical circumstances under which the effect of feebleness could have been greater among the less prominent in the sample—where it is impossible to ascertain—but the incremental effect is not huge and the hypothetical circumstances are highly contingent.[5] On balance converting 5% of testators from marks to signatures would seem ample allowance for the effects of feebleness. This should probably be reduced with time, since testators seem to have made their wills ever farther in advance of death as time passed.[6]

Forgetfulness is another bias associated with aging. As men and especially women grew older, they could have forgotten how to sign their names, though they had once known how. Yet research in the Suffolk, Massachusetts, *Deeds* indicates that no more than 5% of men who attested deeds at age forty-five or older and who were followed through the deeds for at least ten years thereafter switched from signatures to marks.[7] Forgetting in wills would be a little more frequent than among the fifty-five-plus-year-olds followed in the deeds, but it would seem ample to convert 10% of testators from markers to signers to allow for forgetfulness. This was in the seventeenth century when the need to remember literacy was comparatively low and forgetfulness should have been at a maximum. There is some evidence that forgetting decreased as a more complex society put greater demands on individuals.

One further bias slightly lowers the signature rate of older persons relative to the population. In a time of improving educational opportunity, as prevailed throughout much of the western world between the beginning of the seventeenth century and the end of the eighteenth, older persons were at a disadvantage because educational opportunity had improved since they were children and the rest of the population was younger and had been able to benefit from these improvements. The effect of this bias was that sixty-year-old persons leaving wills had a signature rate an absolute 5–10% below the rate for twenty-five-year-olds,[8] although that deficit is reduced to less than 5% when persons leaving wills are compared with the general population, whose average age was over twenty-five. With time the rising trend in signatures began to level off, suggesting a progressive reduction in this bias as well.

While none of these biases is of great moment, their cumulative impact is quite another matter. A best estimate would be that as of 1660 feebleness, forgetfulness, and opportunity lag together could have caused 15% of persons leaving wills to make marks when their counterparts in a group with an age distribution typical of the population would have signed their names.[9] This estimate should be lowered to around 13% for 1710 and 10% for 1760 to allow for some dwindling in the influence of these biases, but these are by no means negligible adjustments.[10]

At least for men, however, wealth and occupation introduce biases with effects opposite to those of age. Men who left wills were nearly twice as wealthy as men who died intestate. Within the sample, wealth has a higher positive correlation with signatures than does any variable.[11] The implication is that the relatively wealthy men who left wills had a higher rate of signatures than did the mass of the male population. Since the correlation between wealth and signatures declined with time, it appears that this bias decreased progressively, yet never to a completely negligible level. Then there is the occupational bias of the sample. A sample which contains on the average less than

10% laborers yet 35% merchants, gentry, professional men, and artisans is clearly biased. The bias could be exaggerated. In America the mass of potential laborers became independent husbandmen, while many farmers who undertook repairs on the side called themselves artisans, and migration itself probably brought New England an unusually high proportion of artisans, merchants, and professionals. The net result was a drastic upward shift in the occupational structure compared with that which had prevailed in England. Nonetheless, it seems doubtful that less than one New Englander in ten was a laborer while over a third of men were in supra-agricultural occupations. Some real higher-occupational bias in the sample must warp it toward an unrepresentative excess of signatures. The correlation of occupation with signatures declined as time passed, steadily lowering the impact of this occupational bias, but never eliminating it completely.

The best way to estimate the degree to which wealth and high occupation inflate the signature rate of the sample is to construct a subsample which conforms closely to the hypothetical distribution of wealth and of occupations among the male population of New England. This has been done. A subsample of 700 men has been selected such that its median wealth is circa £160, £200, £225 in the main periods sampled, to wit 1650–70, 1705–15, 1758–62, as compared with an average of nearly £350 in the raw sample. The occupational distribution has been adjusted by weighting to include 15% laborers in period I, and 20% in periods II and III, and to lower merchants, professionals, gentry, and artisans correspondingly to 20% of the sample in period I and to 15% in periods II and III. This subsample yields signature levels respectively 15%, 10%, and 3% below the levels in the raw sample. These adjustments should probably be somewhat larger, since the men used in the subsample are perhaps still somewhat more wealthy than the male population at large. It might be more accurate to suggest that the high wealth and occupation of the sample give it a signature rate some 20%, 15%, and 5%

[10]

above that of the male population in each respective period. It is doubtful, however, that a larger adjustment should be made.

Thus the opposing biases of age on the one hand and of wealth and occupation on the other appear to have roughly equal and declining impact on the signatures of men leaving wills. In period I the 15% upward adjustment for the effects of age nearly matches the 20% downward adjustment for the "effects" of wealth and occupation. The +13% adjustment for age in period II effectively balances the −15% adjustment for wealth-occupation. The same is true of the respective +10% and −5% figures for period III. The information inherent in the raw data argues against imposing throughout this presentation the small net adjustments which remain.[12]

One bias remains to be discussed. Even controlling for the wealth and occupation biases of the sample, writing a will is itself a selective process. Why did one farmer worth £200 write a will whereas two or three others did not? There is something special about such a man which distinguishes him from his peers, and that quality is almost certainly related to literacy. A person who conceived of the need to control the transmission of property and who followed the forms necessary for legal recognition was more likely to be literate than an equal who died intestate. The result is a powerful bias in favor of signatures in the sample even once all other biases have been adjusted away. It is difficult to measure the impact of this bias,[13] but it means that in the end the signature level of the sample is almost surely above that of the population.

An exception might be noted where the women in the sample are concerned. Women's signatures on wills are subject to a maximum upward adjustment for the effects of feebleness and forgetfulness. It is possible that the effects of these biases declined less among women than among men. Hence it would not be implausible to raise women's signatures by an absolute 15%, 15%, and 12% in each respective period to adjust for the effects of age.[14] At the same time wealth (and of course occupation) does not introduce an equivalent counterbias in the case of women. The correlation between wealth and signatures is only half as strong among women as among men. To continue the hypothetical instance, the downward adjustment called for because of the wealth of women leaving wills would be on the order of only 7.5%, 5%, and 2.5% in each period. This leaves a net upward adjustment of circa 7.5%, 10%, and 9.5% which ought to be made to bring the signature level of women leaving wills up to that of the female population. Those who wish to make this adjustment may. What gives pause is the fact that while one man in three or four left a will only one woman in twenty or thirty left a will. This may be because the only women expected to leave wills were widows. Even so, only one widow in ten left a will.[15] (Nor were these the most wealthy widows, for the overwhelming majority in the sample were of modest means.) The conclusion is that the peculiar selectivity involved in making a will was much more powerful among women than among men. This increment of selectivity among women may be equivalent to the stronger incremental effect of wealth among men, and more than cancel the effects of age on women's signatures.

As far as can be determined in all periods and among both sexes, then, the biases affecting signatures on wills were of moderate force and appear to cancel. This finding, together with the value of presenting the raw data free of small and imprecise adjustments, leads to the informed decision to let signatures on wills represent the signatures of the population.[16] The residual bias of selectivity argues that the male sample was still somewhat higher in signatures than the society, but this remains the best summary of present knowledge. Given that signatures appear to measure literacy, the signatures of the sample can therefore be taken to represent the literacy of the society.

The social correlates of literacy found within this sample do not necessarily, however, describe the correlates of literacy in the population. The sample appears to be repre-

sentative in this respect, but largely because the social correlates of literacy within it are the ones which common
sense would predict in the population.

The Evolution of Literacy in Colonial New England

The evidence is that between the middle of the seventeenth century and the end of the eighteenth New England evolved from a society little more than half-literate
to a society of nearly universal male literacy. This was part
of a slow trend toward higher literacy throughout the
western world, but literacy rose faster and to a higher
level in New England than in most areas.[17] Literacy was
a dynamic variable, and this had its effects on the society.
Yet the social context in which literacy rose, literacy's relationship to human attitudes, and its very extension among
women were all less dynamic than might be thought.

THE first task is to establish the initial level and subsequent trend of male literacy in New England. The raw
data show that as of 1660 only 60% of men signed their
wills, whereas by 1710 the figure had risen to 70% and by
1760 it was up to 85%. Samples from Suffolk and Middlesex Counties, Massachusetts, indicate that male signatures
on wills approached 90% by 1790.[18] So it appears that
after a slow start virtually all men must have been literate
by the end of the eighteenth century, in the sense that they
could read well enough to sign their names and perhaps
to write (Graph 1).[19]

Yet it is one thing to present this trend in the data and
another to defend it. Conventional historians have not predicted such a low initial level of literacy, and, despite all
the methodological assurances already offered, the subsequent trend of male literacy needs some methodological
buttressing.

Previous studies left no room for such an improvement,
for they found a male signature level of 95% as early as

1675. An observer added that "many, perhaps a major part" of the remaining men "could read the King James Bible and other simple English texts." [20] This precocious universal literacy was attributed to the high literacy of the Puritan emigrés and to their famous laws requiring public support of education.[21] The idyll appears, however, to have a weak foundation. The 95% signature rate does not require any adjustment for age, since the petitions and deeds from which it is derived yield a sample of men only slightly older than the male population, but an adjustment must be made for the unusual wealth of the men included in these documents.[22] Investigations indicate a downward adjustment roughly equal to that used for wills, lowering the signature rate from petitions, etc., to 80% to approximate the rate among all males in the society. The remaining discrepancy between the 80% figure and the 60% adjusted figure derived from the wills can be accounted for by scholarly error. It appears that the two previous students of signatures did not control for the repetition of names in their samples. Since literate men recur in documents more frequently than illiterate men, the result is to inflate the proportion of signatures by anywhere from 10% to 30%.[23] Furthermore one of the samples is exclusively from Suffolk County, Massachusetts, whose signature rate was significantly higher than the average for New England. With these inflations removed, previous signature data conform to the estimate of 60% signatures in the male population of seventeeth-century New England.[24] There was indeed room for improvement, as the data indicate.

It is of course fair to ask exactly how many of the 40% of men who could not sign their names could nonetheless read to some degree. Samuel Eliot Morison has suggested "perhaps a major part." [25] This seems reasonable. The schools taught basic reading before writing or even the alphabet, and some parents may have removed their boys from school at this point, on the theory that basic reading was enough for an ordinary man. But this would still leave half of the markers or 20% of all men essentially illiterate. A society in which only 60% of men could read fluently, less than 60% could write, 20% were semi-literate, and 20% were illiterate was a long way from universal male literacy—without mentioning the fact that at this time less than half of women could sign their names.[26]

These data open the way to a new understanding of the respect shown for the sermon, for the minister, and indeed for any highly literate man in seventeenth-century New England. They suggest that New Englanders once lived closer than we have imagined to the credulous word-of-mouth world of the peasant, closer to its absorbing localism, closer to its dependency on tradition and on the informed few. More, the data redefine the task of education in earliest New England. The settlers' task was not to maintain nearly universal literacy in the face of a howling wilderness. Their real job was to continue under the handicaps and advantages of the new environment the ongoing effort to spread literacy, a job the Puritans had already begun in England.[27]

The evidence is that they eventually succeeded, for the subsequent rise in male signatures was as real as the relative illiteracy of the seventeenth century. The rise was not the result of changes in the composition of the sample. Wills represented a constant proportion of the population whose characteristics were largely the same from period to period. Slight increases in the proportion of men with high wealth and occupation and living in urban areas contributed very little to the increase in signatures, and these shifts may have reflected real changes in the population whose effects on signatures should not be removed (Graph 1).[28] Nor was the rise produced only by the peculiarities of persons leaving wills. Lessening feebleness and forgetfulness would have caused the sample's signature level to rise a little faster than the level in the population, but this effect was cancelled by the declining tendency of the sample's wealth to raise its signature rate above that of the population. The sample's relationship to the population remained constant and their rates of increase parallel.[29] It is of course always possible that some unplumbed peculiarity of persons who left wills led to a rise in their rate of signatures while the rate in the population was immobile. Yet a subsample of farmers, whose occupation, poverty, and lack of foresight perhaps made them more typical of the male population, showed the same increase in signatures. There is every reason to believe that the rise in signatures was found among all men.[30]

The rise in signatures was not a rise in "trick" signatures either, i.e., in the proportion of men who were semi-literate or illiterate and who somehow acquired the knack of signing their names. If this knack had been spreading, the proportion of clumsy signatures would have risen, and it did not. The proportion of women signing their names would very likely have risen, and it did not.

The rise in male signatures was not caused by peculiarities of the sample or by "tricks," and it seems to have reflected a general increase in both reading and writing. In theory it could have reflected merely the addition of writing to an elementary curriculum which previously included only reading. Under this circumstance, men who once might have learned to read fluently yet would have been unable to sign their names (unlikely as this sounds) because they had had absolutely no contact with writing in the schools, would increasingly have learned to sign and indeed to write. The rise in signatures would reflect only an increase in writing. This possibility is obviated by the fact that in New England writing had been part of the elementary curriculum from the beginning.[31] A related possibility is more plausible. The rise in signatures could have resulted from a rising inclination on the part of those parents who had sons in school to leave their sons in school longer than the time required to learn basic reading. This would lead to a higher level of signatures which reflected some increase in the quality of reading skills, but primarily an increase in writing skills, and which did not result from an expansion in the proportion of the male

[16]

population exposed to education in literacy. Yet a qualitative increase in reading accompanied by an increase in the proportion of men exposed to education in writing, ultimately affecting on the order of 30% of all males, is by no means a negligible improvement. Where economic development is concerned, writing and the accompanying skill of ciphering are perhaps the most important aspects of literacy. In any event there is no positive evidence that a prolonged attendance alone explains the rise in signatures. It is better to assume that the rise could have stemmed from a variety of sources and that it entailed increases in all aspects of literacy from mere exposure to the alphabet through fluent reading and writing.

The rate of increase in male literacy was not perfectly uniform. The raw rate of increase was nearly twice as rapid after 1710 as before: from exactly 61% signatures circa 1660 to 69% circa 1710 to 84% circa 1760. The most precise measure of rate-of-increase would subject each of the raw figures to the small net adjustments suggested by the estimates of bias, altering 61% to 56% to allow for the −5% net adjustment remaining after balancing a +15% adjustment for the downward biases of age against a −20% adjustment for the upward biases of wealth and occupation, and similarly altering the later figures to 67% (69% adjusted +13% and −15%) and 89% (84% adjusted +10% and −5%). The absolute increase from each of the figures in this 56%-67%-89% sequence to the next figure should then be expressed as a proportion of the preceding figure. From 1660 to 1710 male literacy rose from its initial 56% level by an absolute 11%, thereby rising by an amount equal to 20% of its former level. From 1710 to 1760 male literacy rose from the resulting 67% level by a further absolute 22%, in this case rising by an amount equal to 33% of its former level. By this measure the 20% improvement achieved on the 1660 figure by 1710 is nearly doubled by the 33% improvement achieved on the 1710 figure by 1760. The most precise estimate possible points to the same conclusion as the raw data.

This intensification of the rate of improvement is one of the more important features of the rise in male literacy, and it was more marked than these estimates reveal. Much of the rise in literacy from 1660 to 1710 is associated with modest increases in the wealth, urbanity, etc., of the sample over time. If these effects are removed, by using a 90% subsample which shows no increases, the resulting sequence of literacy rates is 61%, 65%, and 80%. Virtually all of the increase in literacy not associated with rising wealth, etc., took place between 1710 and 1760 (Graph 1).[32] To cast these figures in terms of improvement as a proportion of the preceding level, the 1660 level of 61% improved by only an absolute 4%, equivalent to less than 7% of itself, while the 1710 level of 65% improved by an absolute 15%, an amount equivalent to 23% of itself. By this measure the rate of increase in male literacy was three times as fast after 1710 as before. This higher pace after 1710 is the more impressive considering that the diffusion of literacy tends to meet greater resistance as that skill spreads through the middle ranges of the population and has to reach the last illiterate minority of men. Male literacy rose at three times its former pace against what were probably ever greater obstacles. The rate levelled off thereafter, as would be expected of a variable approaching universality.[33]

The uptrend was, however, fairly uniform spatially. Every area of the New England countryside sampled shows an increase in men's signatures over the years 1660 to 1760. In five of eight areas the rate of improvement was faster after 1710 than before.[34] The remaining three localities show an uptrend which was essentially constant (Graph 2). This uniformity argues that the rise in male literacy was a single event embracing all of New England.

It appears, then, that the evidence of the raw data can be substantiated against previous claims and against methodological caveats. Male literacy indeed began little above the halfway mark, at first advanced very slowly, then rose to the threshold of universality.

Graph 1: Male signatures on New England wills 1650–1795

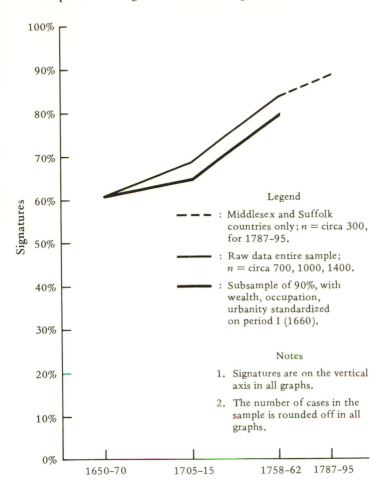

Legend

– – – : Middlesex and Suffolk
       countries only; n = circa 300,
       for 1787–95.

——— : Raw data entire sample;
       n = circa 700, 1000, 1400.

▬▬▬ : Subsample of 90%, with
       wealth, occupation,
       urbanity standardized
       on period I (1660).

Notes

1. Signatures are on the vertical
   axis in all graphs.

2. The number of cases in the
   sample is rounded off in all
   graphs.

[19]

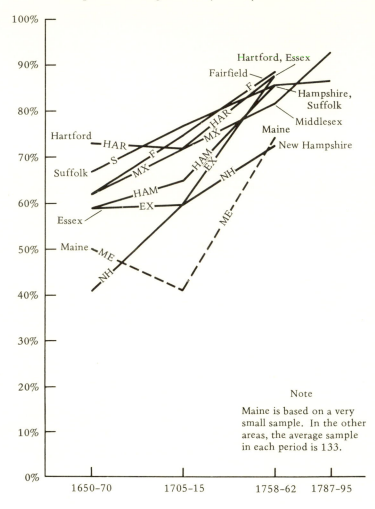

Graph 2: Male signatures by county over time

THE advent of universal male literacy had one inevitable consequence. The movement toward universal literacy was essentially a movement of previously less literate groups and regions to a state of widespread literacy heretofore found only among their social superiors, and the advance of these groups virtually erased the statistical association of literacy with high social status.[35]

Specifically, the emergence of universal male literacy was the result of a sharp increase in rural literacy, especially in the literacy of back-country farmers. Boston was three-quarters literate to begin with and whether there or in the countryside the merchants, gentry, and professionals were almost entirely literate from the outset. If male literacy was going to improve substantially, there would have to be a sharp improvement among the rural farmers, artisans, and laborers who made up more than three-quarters of the male population and who were little more than half-literate (Graphs 3, 4). This is exactly what happened; very nearly all of the increase in male literacy is accounted for by these groups.[36] Farmers are the best example, since they alone accounted for over half the sample and almost three-quarters of the society. Their literacy rose from 45% in 1660 to 60% in 1710 to 80% in 1760, nearly doubling in a century, moving at a rate faster than that for the male sample as a whole. In some areas farmer literacy surpassed 85% by 1790. Here again a slight increase in the wealth of the successive samples is not the cause of the rising trend in signatures. Once the distribution of wealth in the second, third, and fourth samples of farmers is made identical to the distribution in the first (by discarding), the signature rates are still 45%, 56%, 78%, and 83%.[37]

The result of the powerful rise in farmer literacy to levels ultimately approaching 85%, and of comparable long-term increases among rural artisans and laborers, was a male literacy so nearly universal that it effectively ended old associations between literacy and social distinctions. Regional distinctions lost a dimension of reality as regional differences in literacy evaporated. While Boston moved slowly if at all above its original three-quarters male literacy, rural New England rose out of half-literacy, first to equal then perhaps to surpass the level of the city (Graph 3). The countryside could no longer be scorned by city slickers certain that any farmer they ran into would likely as not be an illiterate "pumpkin." The more backwoods the area the more rapid was its rate of improvement, until there were no backwoods of literacy left. In 1660, Maine and New Hampshire had a male literacy below 50% as compared with 60% for Essex and Hampshire Counties and 70% for the capital counties of Suffolk, Massachusetts, and Hartford, Connecticut (Graph 2). A hundred years later Maine and New Hampshire had risen to 75% literacy and the other localities were clustered tightly around 85%. The characteristics of far rural New England—the illiteracy of its first settlers, its relative poverty, low density, and lack of sophistication—no longer entailed the added disgrace of mass illiteracy or even relative illiteracy.[38]

Similarly, distinctions in occupational status no longer created or were reinforced by substantial differences in literacy. As of 1660 the "upper crust" of merchants, professional men, and gentry had been entirely literate while artisans hovered above and farmers below half-literacy (Graph 4).[39] One reason was that literacy was necessary to high status careers while it was dispensable in other vocations. Yet the result was that superior status carried a certainty of literacy while social inferiority was often reaffirmed by illiteracy. The surge in rural literacy erased these associations as surely as it had dissipated the links between regional distinctions and literacy. Men became literate regardless of their occupations and the result was that, while in 1760 the rank order of literacy rates still matched that of social status, the differences in literacy were so small that literacy barely echoed the continuing distinctions of status.[40]

The association between status and literacy had been strengthened by an association between wealth and literacy.

This relationship was independent of the link between occupational needs and literacy. For example, in 1660, 60% of farmers worth more than £400 had been literate as against 45% of farmers worth less.[41] For generations wealth had sought or bought literacy and literacy had earned wealth, until the two were so inextricably linked that literacy helped maintain the aura of superiority attached to wealth. Rising literacy nearly erased these associations as well. Men of all estates became literate, until farmers worth less than £400 were fully as literate (82%) as farmers worth more. The least wealthy men still showed a significant proportion of illiterates, but even their literacy was rising rapidly (Graph 5).[42] Wealth and occupation still distinguished one man from another, basic literacy rarely did.

The rise in literacy begins to look like a *deus ex machina*, arising even in a subsample whose wealth does not increase and acting most powerfully among less wealthy regions and groups of men, to end the ancient association of literacy with social distinctions. These regions and men had farthest to go, so the unknown forces behind educational progress inevitably had most effect there, but the important point is that some forces not directly dependent on wealth pervaded every corner of New England to make literacy universal. Thanks to these forces education became widely available, if it had not been so before, and now even the meanest of men took advantage of its accessibility. At the same time, the god from the machine had its limitations. The forces which were raising literacy in New England did not necessarily involve the expectation of social opportunity. As will be seen, the mere availability of education, or piety, or necessity, may have been the motives which led men increasingly to attend to the education of their sons. Concerning the reality of opportunity, there was no major upward shift in occupational structure or in per capita wealth after 1710, at least within the sample. This implies not only that the rise in literacy was not a

Graph 3: Male signatures, Boston v. Rural, over time

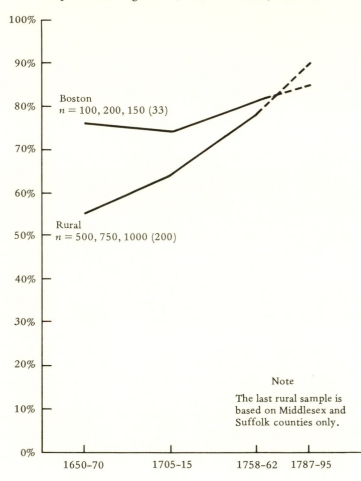

Boston
$n = 100, 200, 150\ (33)$

Rural
$n = 500, 750, 1000\ (200)$

Note

The last rural sample is
based on Middlesex and
Suffolk counties only.

1650–70   1705–15   1758–62   1787–95

Graph 4: Male signature rate by occupation

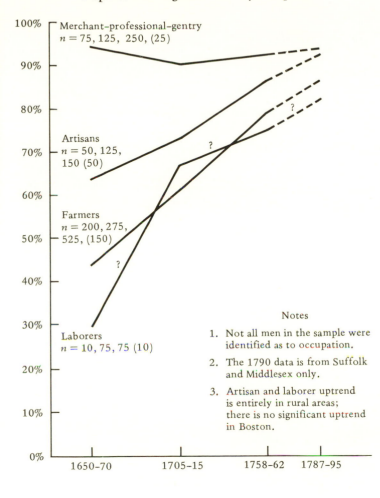

Merchant–professional–gentry
n = 75, 125, 250, (25)

Artisans
n = 50, 125, 150 (50)

Farmers
n = 200, 275, 525, (150)

Laborers
n = 10, 75, 75 (10)

Notes

1. Not all men in the sample were identified as to occupation.

2. The 1790 data is from Suffolk and Middlesex only.

3. Artisan and laborer uptrend is entirely in rural areas; there is no significant uptrend in Boston.

1650–70   1705–15   1758–62   1787–95

LIBRARY
OF
MOUNT ST. MARY'S
COLLEGE
EMMITSBURG, MARYLAND

[25]

Graph 5: Male signatures by wealth over time

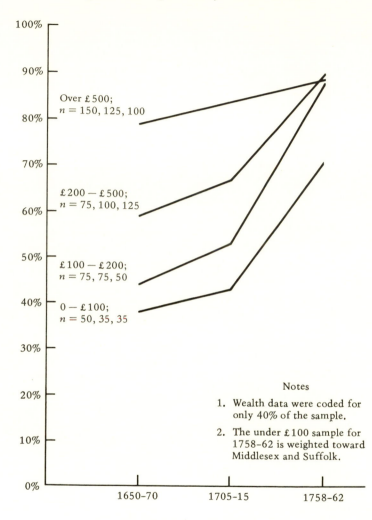

Over £500;
$n = 150, 125, 100$

£200 — £500;
$n = 75, 100, 125$

£100 — £200;
$n = 75, 75, 50$

0 — £100;
$n = 50, 35, 35$

Notes

1. Wealth data were coded for only 40% of the sample.

2. The under £100 sample for 1758–62 is weighted toward Middlesex and Suffolk.

1650–70   1705–15   1758–62

result of improving social conditions, but that rising literacy did not lead to relatively improved social and economic conditions for the men who newly acquired this skill.

There remained, too, a hard core of illiterate men for whom the old associations between literacy and status were as valid as ever. Even in 1760, certain occupations required literacy. Illiterates did not possess this skill so their occupational mobility was limited. Probably because relatively poor fathers had bequeathed them both small inheritances and the handicap of illiteracy, as well as because their level of congenital incompetence was high, the residual illiterates averaged less than half the wealth of literates. The result was that illiterates were so concentrated among laborers and among men worth less than £100 that membership in these groups still carried a high possibility of illiteracy (Graph 5).

Thus the forces which reached so deeply into this society did not necessarily involve changes in the expectation or in the reality of social opportunity, nor did they reach absolutely every man. *Within these limits* the social structure of literacy had been transformed as male literacy rose toward universality. Seventeenth-century New England had been a half-literate society in which literacy correlated with cosmopolitan status and with wealth. Slowly, then more rapidly, remarkably pervasive forces increased the literacy of distant and less prominent men until the meanest orders of men were three-quarters literate and yeoman farmers were near universal literacy. Literacy became the basic condition of men in New England.

LITERACY, the growth of literacy, and the end of its class structure are statistical events. They are real, but say nothing about the minds of men in this society. To seek the conscious impact of literacy, and of the growth of literacy, it will be necessary to enter the realm of social theorizers.

Social scientists have observed that literacy is sometimes associated with changes in the ways men view the world, particularly when other changes are taking place within a society. This appears to be the case in what was formerly East Pakistan.[43] Here, literates are significantly more enthusiastic about higher education and about new methods of cultivation than are illiterates.[44] This may betoken an emergence from traditional fatalism, an increased willingness to take action, and an optimistic expectation of success. It could also bespeak an awareness of a world beyond the village, a world with forces which will make education and innovation ever more helpful. Awareness of this wider world shows itself in the greater tendency of literates to identify themselves not with the village or tribe but with the new nation. Literates tend not only to perceive but to give their loyalty to these large abstractions. Further impact of literacy on attitudes seems to require urban settings in which mass media and their socializing influences operate on literate men, and even in this setting "rather than literacy [being] a factor which completely pervades and shapes a man's entire view of the world, [it is] limited to those spheres where vicarious and abstract experience is especially meaningful." [45] These limitations notwithstanding, literate men tend to be nearer than their illiterate brethren to a "modern" personality type which is emerging in this as in other developing nations. The activism, optimism, awareness of wider forces, and the larger loyalties shown by literates are precisely the qualities which distinguish this modern personality. Literacy is therefore clearly involved with the larger social processes which are evolving this personality.[46]

Several historians have implied that this kind of social process was at work in colonial America. One has suggested that colonial education enhanced "typical American individualism, optimism, and enterprise" by focusing upon the student the diversity and mobility increasingly characteristic of early American society.[47] Since everyone exposed to this educational ethos must have acquired literacy while being socialized, if not indeed required literacy for that process, there should be an ever stronger positive correlation between literacy and the individualistic, optimistic, and enterprising attitudes enhanced by the schools. Illiterates would show such attitudes only to a lesser degree. Another historian explicitly asserts that by the eighteenth century American literacy had a "liberated" quality, primarily because literate men were exposed to schools and newspapers, which socialized them in the emerging diversity, mobility, and participatory consciousness of the colonial scene. Literate men were "liberated" in that they were participatory, and aware of wider issues and loyalties, presumably more so than illiterates.[48]

The processes described by these historians are very similar to the process of socialization which appears to have led to the modernization of attitudes in East Pakistan.[49] In both cases literacy is intimately involved in an educational subprocess which enhances the changes in attitudes already encouraged by general changes in the society. In both instances, the results are a more active, instrumental, optimistic, and widely aware consciousness particularly associated with literacy.

COULD this have been happening in colonial New England? If it was, the substantial increase in literacy must have meant a large increase in the proportion of men most likely to espouse the new attitudes evoked by the development of the society—individualism, optimism, enterprise.

If the social context was such as to encourage the development of "liberated" attitudes, particularly through literacy, exactly what might have been the further implications of this development as amplified by the rise in literacy which took place in eighteenth-century New England? It could be said that the advent of universal literacy would have increased both the unity of men and their contentiousness, in a paradox typical of the modernization of attitudes.

In the first place, the homogenization of literacy at a high level among almost all classes may have had certain unifying effects. We think of social development as a process which divides men, an assumption implicit in the term "social differentiation." Yet here would be an instance in which social development created the opposite of differentiation, a unification of human skills following ages of hierarchical differentiation. Mass literacy removed one traditional measure of the distinction between town and country and in the country between gentleman and farmer and between rich farmer and poor. Dependency on "others" for information or communication lessened apace. To the degree that these changes reduced respectively men's awareness of differences between men and their suspicions of men who were different, mass literacy unified men in consciousness as well as in fact. More, by giving all men access to the same basic sources of information, mass literacy made it technically more feasible for men to be unified quickly and on a large scale around a common loyalty.

More importantly, mass literacy would not only have created a world in which men's disunities were lessened and in which men could more easily be reached by appeals to unity, it would also have increased the proportion of men responsive to such appeals. For in the proper contexts the literate man tends to be more aware of wider unities among men than is his illiterate counterpart. It is not clear whether literacy actually produces such attitudes, but this is plausible since literacy exposes men to the socializing agencies which initiate them into a world outside their localities. In any event, in the case study cited literate men were more likely to identify with a new nation than were illiterates, whose identities still lay with their villages or regions. And there is a hint that literates looked more to purely political leaders who embodied this new unity than to village leaders endowed with the traditional superiorities. These unifying "effects" of literacy would have existed within colonial New England as well as in modernizing nations today. Thus the shift of nearly a third of New England male society from illiteracy to literacy implied an increase in the proportion of men who were responsive to wider loyalties than those in their villages.

One result might be seen in the response of the New England countryside to the appeals for patriotic unity sent out by the Boston Committee of Correspondence during the revolutionary crisis of the 1770's.[50] Traditionally suspicious of the city, the country nonetheless responded to a tide of letters, pamphlets, and public appeals. A unified revolutionary movement emerged behind the Boston radicals as they provoked the repressive measures which brought colonists elsewhere into a war for independence. Could the Boston Committee have succeeded if more than half the farmers of New England had remained illiterate? Dependent upon their sometimes cautious superiors for information, and unhearing in their suspicion of rumored Boston, illiterate farmers would have made a bad audience for a revolution whose issues were often abstracted beyond the local experience. As it was, a literate countryside rallied with unexpected speed. The larger psychological world of the literate man could embrace a novel abstraction called "America," whereas to illiterates the new nation would have been a shadow filtered through local hearsay, as indeed was more the case in the less literate South where Toryism was also stronger.

At the same time the very experiences which made literate New Englanders see beyond the locality could also have led them into increased political contentiousness. As they became aware of a world outside their villages, literate men also come to believe more strongly than their illiterate cousins in taking individual action to remedy problems. Rising literacy could therefore have entailed an increase in the proportion of men who had shed passive acceptance of the status quo in favor of political action to gain their own ends. In modern culture this is an accustomed response, but it could have raised unprecedented hell in eighteenth-century New England. This is particularly true because universal literacy had not eliminated all the divisions between men. To the contrary, interregional and interpersonal differences of status and wealth had never been greater.[51] In this situation mass literacy may have encouraged as well as been a tool in the hands of groups and regions resenting their relative inferiority.

Thus mass literacy could have fueled the notorious contentiousness of late eighteenth-century New England as well as fostered its unity in the national cause. The paradoxes of Yankee behavior may have been the paradox of modern attitudes writ early, and the immediate impact of contentiousness may have been more meaningful to New Englanders than their visions of unity.

YET is it correct to assume that eighteenth-century New England was a society in which a modernization of attitudes could occur, in which literacy enhanced these attitudes, and in which an increase in literacy swelled the tide of modern views?

There are several hints that it was not. As mentioned, the rise in literacy and concomitant evaporation of its class structure did not occur in a context of rising real opportunity. The wealth and occupational structures in the sample changed little at the very time literacy was rising most radically. Some force was present sufficient to raise male literacy, but the data raise the question whether in general this society was dynamic enough to sustain the kind of social processes associated with the modernization of attitudes.

Further doubt arises from Horace Mann's subsequent complaints that the New England educational system was not meeting the needs of the industrializing nineteenth century. The system was still producing mass literacy, as it had begun to do in the eighteenth century, yet Mann felt that this alone was not a sufficient human resource for advanced economic development in New England. Additional skills and above all attitudes were required. Mann called for an end to the fecklesness of rural schools and for an effort to produce new attitudes in the work force. Such views make it difficult to believe that a modernization of attitudes had already taken place in New England.[52]

The wills of the men in this sample tend to confirm the suspicion that no modernization of attitudes occurred in colonial New England. It is possible to measure the attitudes of these men in several ways. Did a man leave all of his estate to his family or did he think of the larger needs of society? If the latter, was his concern directed to persons near to his family, to other persons within his home village, to more abstract causes within his village, or outward to causes in the world beyond the village? To what purpose did he leave his gifts; were they the traditional alms to alleviate the suffering of the poor or testify to his concern for religion; or was there an effort to rehabilitate the poor, or to educate men, or to improve the condition of their environment? These measures do not match precisely the "modern" man found in Pakistan, nor do they exactly reflect the "individualistic, enterprising, optimistic" not to mention "liberated" American which some historians suppose existed by the middle eighteenth century. Yet these measures come close enough that they should change in response to any massive increase in the proportion of men, literate or illiterate, who were "modern" in the ways described by social scientists and historians. If these were the trends of the times, then all men in the sample but particularly literate men should show an increasing tendency to give to the needs of society, and particularly to give outside the environs of the family, to give to abstract causes rather than to persons, to give outside the home village, and to give to rehabilitative rather than to alleviative ends. Such would be expected of active, widevisioned, and optimistic men, and from the evidence such choices were available.

No such changes took place, probably because the choices were not compelling. Any modernization of attitudes did not show its activism, optimism, and wider consciousness in a heightened level of charitable concern. The rate of giving to charity within the sample declined significantly from the middle of the seventeenth century to the end of the eighteenth. The decline was the same among literates as among illiterates. Literates tended always to give at a higher level than illiterates, but, once the extra wealth of literates is removed, the two groups show identical levels of giving sloping downwards together. It is possible that there was a widespread change in attitudes and that its "individualistic" component prevailed over its wide-visioned optimistic activism, thereby reducing bequests to society. Yet there seem to be other explanations of the decline in charitable giving. It is most logical to assume that there was simply no attitudinal change sufficient to move men in general or literates in particular to greater action on behalf of their fellow men.

Among men who did give to charity, the tendency was to find the focus of charity in a person connected with the family, in some other person within the village, or at best in an abstract cause still within the village. Gifts to causes outside the village were extremely rare. As Table 1 shows, this was as true in the age of universal literacy as it had been a century before.

Table 1

	GIFTS TO A PERSON WITHIN THE VILLAGE CONNECTED WITH THE FAMILY (SERVANTS).	GIFTS TO A PERSON WITHIN THE VILLAGE NOT CONNECTED WITH THE FAMILY (MINISTERS).	GIFTS TO A CAUSE WITHIN THE VILLAGE (THE POOR, RELIGION, EDUCATION).	GIFTS TO A CAUSE OUTSIDE THE VILLAGE (THE POOR, RELIGION, EDUCATION).
Gifts*	42	211	139	23
1650–1715	10%	49%	35%	6%
		n = 414 gifts		
Gifts*	28	39	86	5
1758–95	17%	25%	55%	3%
		n = 158 gifts		

* (Literates and non-literates combined.)

In the eighteenth century an increased proportion of all gifts went to persons connected with the giver's family. While there was a modest increase in the awareness of abstract causes, this did not extend to a greater consciousness of needs outside the village. This remained a world of persons nearly as much as of abstractions, and overwhelmingly a local world. The persistence of the traditional foci of giving was as characteristic of literates as it was of illiterates. For example:

Table 2

	GIFTS TO A PERSON WITHIN THE VILLAGE CONNECTED WITH THE FAMILY (SERVANTS).	GIFTS TO A PERSON WITHIN THE VILLAGE NOT CONNECTED WITH THE FAMILY (MINISTERS).	GIFTS TO A CAUSE WITHIN THE VILLAGE (THE POOR, RELIGION, EDUCATION).	GIFTS TO A CAUSE OUTSIDE THE VILLAGE (THE POOR, RELIGION, EDUCATION).
Gifts by literates 1758–95	23 17%	32 24%	75 55%	5 4%
		n = 135 gifts		
Gifts by illiterates 1758–95	5 20%	7 30%	11 50%	0 0
		n = 23 gifts		

The aggregate therefore does not hide a process of attitudinal change associated only with literacy. The world of human concern remained a personal, and above all a local, world for all of these New Englanders.

The purposes of charitable giving likewise remained traditional. Most men in all periods gave in order to alleviate the needs of the poor or to further religion. With rare exceptions none of these gifts involved any attempt to rehabilitate the poor or to turn religion to constructive secular needs. Only a tiny proportion of gifts went to educate men or to municipal improvements. This proportion did not increase with time.

Table 3

	GIFTS TO THE POOR.	GIFTS TO RELIGION, MINISTERS.	GIFTS TO EDUCATION.	GIFTS TO MUNICIPALITIES.
Gifts	104	283	48	4
1650–1715	23.7%	64.5%	10.9%	0.9%
		n = 439*		
Gifts	54	91	17	2
1758–95	32.9%	55.5%	10.4%	1.2%
		n = 164*		

* Note: some gifts impossible to classify under the previous measure can be classified on this scale, hence the larger numbers.

The eighteenth-century aggregate does not hide a trend to rehabilitative giving on the part of literates alone. The purposes to which literates and illiterates gave were so nearly identical that another table would be superfluous.

If there was an attitudinal "modernization" in eighteenth-century New England it did not increase these men's action in behalf of their fellows, nor did it raise their eyes far from personal or at all from local needs, nor did it move them from their traditional motives of alleviation and piety. Literate men remained as unmoved as their illiterate fellows, as deeply embedded in the locality and in the ancient motives, despite whatever forces education focused upon them. Evidently the social context was not such as to generate changes in the quality of attitudes, even in association with literacy, so the massive increase in the quantity of literacy did not enlarge the pool of new attitudes in this society.[53, 54]

MASS literacy did equip all men with a basic skill of life,

but in the end the spread of this minimal skill may have proven a frustratingly empty achievement. In the seventeenth century many men had been illiterate, but the times had barely required literacy. Most transactions were local face-to-face affairs. Land was customarily obtained from the town by grant and, despite the law, deeds were registered with the community more often than in the county court. The gap between the literacy of the population and the functional demands of the society was not great. A century later, in spite of universal male literacy, this gap may have been greater. In the more complex society of the later eighteenth century land was obtained by purchase, often from an entrepreneur, and deeds were registered in the county court. More men lived by commerce, and fewer by semi-subsistence farming. The political challenges of the Revolution required voters to decide issues more intricate than had ever been placed before the public. Basic reading and writing were only the beginning of the demands the times placed upon men. If the eighteenth century saw a spread of basic literacy without much improvement in its quality, men may have been further than ever from the skills needed to function independently.

Contentiousness may have been increased as a consequence of this literacy gap, but it would not have been so much the contentiousness of modern man as the ages-old frustration of men unable to deal with a changing world. From this perspective whatever modernization of attitudes resulted from the spread of basic literacy would be minor in comparison with the growing inability of New Englanders to comprehend the world. New England's farmers would have resembled their less literate counterparts throughout the colonies, passive before or frustrated by an environment changing beyond their comprehension. Neither mass literacy nor, in all the colonies, the Revolution could alter this frustration. The record sustains the argument, for throughout the Revolution rural Americans complained of dark doings they could not understand, and pleaded for a return to a world without commercial mysteries. In the long run the level of basic literacy in the colonies, and the advent of mass literacy in New England may appear of little relevance in the face of a society whose demands far outpaced what either colonial literacy or colonial culture prepared men to understand.[55]

COLONIAL New England provided a better climate for women's literacy than had prevailed among the first settlers. Only a third of the women who died before 1670 could sign their names, whereas nearly 45% of the women who died throughout the rest of the colonial and early national eras left signatures on their wills.[56] This new climate seems to have emerged late in the seventeenth century, when opportunities for women's education may have been improving as fast as those for men and women's literacy first approached the 45% level (Graph 6).

But thereafter, within this improved climate, there was no significant further rise in women's signatures.[57] In part this is because there are too few women in the sample to make the ensuing rise on the graph statistically reliable. But a larger sample might include more ordinary women with a lower and more stagnant level of signatures. There could, of course, have been an increase in women's ability to read which was not reflected in signatures, but alternately the rise in signatures which occurred could have been an increase in skilled forgeries by illiterate housewives. On balance it seems that there was no more than a very slow rise in women's literacy after it reached the 40% level around the turn of the eighteenth century.[58]

At the moment when male literacy accelerated toward universality women's literacy stagnated below the halfway level. The resulting counterpoint was most dramatic in the countryside, where women may have lost ground from the beginning and where the divergence of literacy rates early in the eighteenth century appears to have been most distinct (Graph 7).[59] At the outset only a third of women were literate but only half of men were literate and less than half of farmers. Rural women shared the handi-

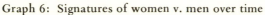

Graph 6: Signatures of women v. men over time

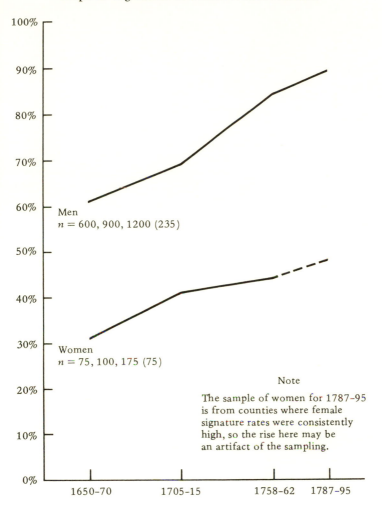

Men
$n = 600, 900, 1200\ (235)$

Women
$n = 75, 100, 175\ (75)$

Note

The sample of women for 1787–95
is from counties where female
signature rates were consistently
high, so the rise here may be
an artifact of the sampling.

1650–70   1705–15   1758–62   1787–95

Graph 7: Signatures of rural men v. rural women over time

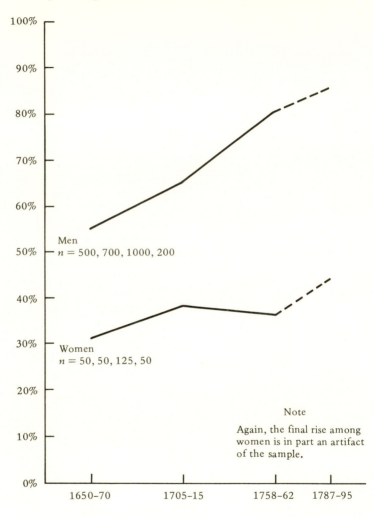

Men
$n = 500, 700, 1000, 200$

Women
$n = 50, 50, 125, 50$

Note

Again, the final rise among women is in part an artifact of the sample.

Graph 8: Women's signatures, Boston v. rural, over time

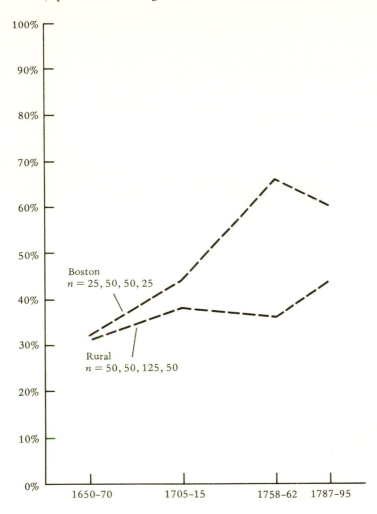

Boston
$n = 25, 50, 50, 25$

Rural
$n = 50, 50, 125, 50$

cap of mass illiteracy with their men. A century later only a little more than a third of rural women were literate whereas more than twice as many rural men were literate and male illiteracy was becoming rare. The rise in male literacy had left in its wake some laborers, some poor men, and most women. The changes in rural New England did not reach to this last refuge of illiteracy and to this last target of the condescension it evoked.

Graph 8 indicates that such continuing increase as there was in women's literacy took place in Boston. Only in this intensely urban atmosphere did women's opportunities continue to improve until more than half of them were literate. Even in Boston there may have remained a large gap between male literacy and the literacy achieved by women in the second half of the eighteenth century.[60] As with the other aspects of literacy, the changes in women's literacy went only so far, and in the case of women's literacy it was not very far at all.

The relative inertia of women's literacy was the result of intention on the part of this culture. Women were discriminated against because they were women, not because they were poor: men who had as little wealth as the women in the sample were 80% literate while their female companions in poverty were only 45% literate. In its deliberate discrimination against women New England proclaimed its allegiance to tradition.[61]

NEW ENGLAND experienced a rise in literacy which erased the statistical association between this skill and social status and achieved universal male literacy before the industrial age. At the same time it did not measure up to the achievements implicitly assigned by some American historians. New England was initially far less literate than has been claimed, literacy rose slowly at first, and it is not clear that the eventual rise to universal male literacy was part of a dynamic social context which involved improving opportunity or which created "modern" men who dealt optimistically with the world outside their villages. In addition, women's literacy may have risen more slowly than men's, reaching little above the halfway mark, and there was a continuing relative discrimination against women in the educational ethos.

If more has been expected of New England, it is because of an implicit assumption that early American society was suffused with powerful forces which everywhere raised literacy to high levels and associated it with new attitudes. The data on literacy in New England suggest some limitations to this assumption. Here where the "dynamism of American society" was augmented by Puritan concern for education, literacy barely rose for quite a long time and remained in some ways rather traditional.[62]

The Sources of Literacy in Colonial New England

An enquiry into the causes of the rise in male literacy in New England suggests that this was in fact a rather different social world from that of "American" dynamism. The source of such change as there was in literacy appears to lie solely in the intentions of the Puritan migrants. Insofar as literacy moved, it was for reasons associated with their ideology, an ideology which had no intention of revolutionizing literacy further.

The prevailing hypothesis holds that Americans responded to the dissolving effects of the wilderness with a uniquely conscious desire to protect the transmission of culture through formal provisions for education. In New England the settlers' concern reinforced an existing Puritan respect for education. The result was the famous New England school laws requiring public support of schools. Presumably these laws were quite effective in maintaining or expanding an extremely high literacy which prevailed among the migrants, though in the eighteenth century population dispersal may have caused a slight decline in their impact. The "frenzied" response to the wilderness which underlay these laws was a driving force in educational improvements elsewhere in America. This widespread reaction to the wilderness ultimately combined with social mobility and social diversification to produce everywhere in colonial America an educational ethos which was a powerful force for social change, and as well a source of "typical" American optimism, individualism, and enterprise. Such an hypothesis would seem to imply a rising and fairly high level of literacy everywhere in eighteenth-century America, as a product of the dynamic impulses involved and as a means of access to the positive attitudes it entailed.[63]

The evidence from New England points to an alternative causal hypothesis which is more consistent with the actual achievements of this region. In reality the wilderness was never much of a threat to maintaining the moderate levels of literacy and of concomitant socialization which prevailed among the settlers of New England. Only a few rhetoricians perceived such a threat, and the Puritan concern for education proved ample to counter any danger and slowly to expand literacy. If the wilderness had a role it was first to offer unusual scope to the Puritan concern for education then initially to delay its full impact on society. "Emigration [to America] enabled the Puritans to carry out in education, as in religion, the system which they thought best." [64] The result was to expand their concern for education into the famous school laws, an immensely powerful means of achieving their ends. Education in general and literacy in particular should have spread at a very rapid pace. Yet at first literacy did not spread at all rapidly. One consequence was that for a long time a traditional European causal structure determined who in New England would be literate and who would be illiterate. Only after half a century under the school laws did literacy finally increase at the expected pace and erase this old causal structure. The reason for the delay seems to be simply that the population of earliest New England was not sufficiently concentrated for the school laws to have full effect. As the population became more concentrated schooling was more widely available and the need for literacy more generally evident. In this sense the wilderness or rather the frontier conditions of earliest New England were a handicap yet only in that they served to delay the triumph of that Puritan educational tradition to which America had seemed to offer unusual scope.

Protestantism, then, lay behind the eventual advance in male literacy in colonial New England. With such a motive at work it was to be expected that the attitudes of literate men remained traditional and that women did not improve their relative educational position. This was a world of the past. Within this more subdued world it is possible to hold great respect for the Protestant impulse as the sole force powerful enough to work a transformation in the level of literacy. This religion has, perhaps justifiably, been seen as an ideology which paved the way to modernity. It is possible, too, to consider lesser social forces which interacted with the Protestant impulse and which independently gave rise to some variations in the level of literacy. Yet in the end this appears to be quite another world from that suggested elsewhere.

The evidence will not prove that the alternative hypothesis offered here explains the evolution of literacy in New England. It merely suggests that this hypothesis may explain the evolution of literacy within the sample and that this possibility opens the door to a more realistic view of the forces involved with literacy in colonial New England.[65]

THE initial level of literacy had little to do with the educational environment of New England. Most persons dying circa 1660 were educated before the migration to America, typically around 1615.[66] If 60% of men and 30% of women were literate, we must look to early seventeenth-century England for the causes.

England was at this time one of the most literate nations in the world.[67] The generation of men educated early in the seventeenth century showed a literacy rate of over 33% as compared with estimates of perhaps 20% for Scotland or France. With Wales excluded, the English rate may have been higher still. In explaining the literacy of the initial sample we must first ask why the base rate of literacy was especially high in England. The only reflections to date assign some weight to the growth of the gentry and perhaps to the desire to rise into this class. There is also mention of a certain social tolerance of lower-class literacy. Most weight, however, is placed upon the Protestant impulse. Protestants were convinced that access to the Word would free men from superstition, and it seems that the gathered groups of devotees responded by providing for the education of their young.

Still, the rate of male literacy among the arrivals in New England was nearly double the base rate prevailing in England. How to explain this? Regional variations within England were substantial, and the eastern regions whence many migrants came had a male literacy closer to 50%. This, however, is not sufficient explanation by itself. The degree and momentum of commercial involvement and above all of Puritan sentiment probably explain why these regions were more literate. In the same vein, a substantial proportion of the migrants came from the West and the North, where male literacy was lower than the English average.[68] It is likely that migrants from these areas were drawn from a Puritan minority which had a higher rate of literacy than the population. The most reasonable explanation, then, is that the migrants were part of a Puritan subpopulation which was concentrated in the eastern counties but could be found elsewhere and whose literacy was substantially above the level prevailing in England.

It is not certain that this fully explains the level of literacy among the arrivals.[69] Swedish scholars have established that within eligible populations it is the literates who are most likely to move.[70] Perhaps within the Puritan population the chance to emigrate selected an unusually literate group. In this light the migrants' literacy was the product of a long process of refinement.[71]

The initial differences in literacy between regions of New England arose because of differences in the literacy rates within the stream of migrants. It could hardly be otherwise when the persons in the sample were educated in England. Connecticut seems to have fared a little better than Massachusetts, possibly because its settlers included strongly motivated re-emigrants from Massachusetts and highly commercialized Puritans from London. Both colonies received migrants considerably more literate than those in New Hampshire and Maine (Graph 2). The level of literacy in these peripheral settlements was nearly as low as in England, potentially because a large proportion of non-Puritans was mixed into this migrant substream.

These differences persisted into the next period. The rank-order of counties by literacy rate was nearly the same in 1710 as fifty years before (Graph 2).[72] This raises an interesting point, for without this evidence the regional differences in 1710 would seem to be the result of a blend of social development with school laws. Sophisticated Suffolk was followed by Fairfield, already an economic suburb of New York. They were trailed by rather more primitive counties which nonetheless basked in the benefits of the school laws, and the tail was occupied by wild and lawless New Hampshire. Such arguments must reckon with the evidence that the determinant of these regional variations in literacy was the original variation in the literacy of the migrant substreams.[73]

In most cases all causal forces would flow toward the existing rank-order of literacies, so one can only observe that it may not have been only social sophistication and school laws which placed Connecticut near the top but also the high literacy of its settlers. Likewise the low rank of New Hampshire and Maine may not be attributable solely to wilderness conditions and a lack of schools but also to the low level of literacy among the settlers of these areas. Essex County, Massachusetts, however, shows that inheritance could have been the stronger determinant. As of 1710 Essex had enjoyed a full reign of school laws and was developing into one of the more urbanized counties within Massachusetts. Yet its literacy level ranked below the rest of Massachusetts. The explanation seems to lie in the fact that the original settlers of this county were distinctly less literate than the rest of the migrants who flooded into Massachusetts and Connecticut. This test case suggests that the literacy of the migrants was indeed the most powerful source of the regional variations in literacy which prevailed early in the eighteenth century.

To the degree that this is valid, the wilderness was not the real culprit in the low achievements of northern New England, nor were school laws the real source of higher achievements elsewhere. For this period the negative impact of the frontier has been overrated, as has the positive impact of school laws. As of 1710 the rank-order of local literacy was simply the rank-order of the settlers' literacy, and the scholar is left to search into the nearly unmeasurable processes by which parents transmitted their education to their children.[74] Ironically, these processes were once supposed to have collapsed under the impact of the frontier and generally to have been replaced by school laws which did the job better. It appears that these processes simply endured.

This is not to say that the new environment had no effect on literacy. The point is that in 1710 one locality's literacy achievements relative to another may not have been determined so much by variations in wilderness conditions or in school laws as by the orderly transmission of literacy from its inhabitants' progenitors.

A CLOSER look at the settlers' reactions confirms this indication that neither the wilderness nor responses to it were real forces on the scene. Unconcerned about the wilderness, the Puritans simply passed some school laws out of traditional motives. These were not fully effective in the dispersed population, and literacy continued to be transmitted largely unchanged in its local variations and in its overall level.

"Orderly" best describes the settlers' reactions to the new environment. Evidently the wilderness had little impact on family life, for these pioneers held their families together so successfully that relatively few sons left home in search of an independent existence. This traditional context for education was preserved if not actually strengthened.[75] Moreover, nothing in the settlers' wills suggests a "frenzied" effort to forestall the dissolving effects of the wilderness on traditional culture by providing for formal education. In New England as in New York and in Virginia only 5–10% of settlers' wills mentioned education at all. Virtually none of these said a word about a threatening wilderness directly or indirectly. The level of solicitude was about the same as in England and similarly the usual provision simply left a sum to pay for a child's education.[76]

If there is any remaining suspicion that the wilderness was a threat, the subsequent record of backwoods areas should dispel all doubt. While literacy in general barely rose, literacy in backwoods New Hampshire and Hampshire County actually rose at a slightly faster rate than elsewhere. Similarly farmers, the group supposedly most exposed to the erosions of the raw environment, showed significant progress while other occupations did not. As the Puritans seem to have known from the beginning, there was little to fear in the wilderness, even in such areas as New Hampshire which did not have school laws.[77] It is in this context that one can understand why New World conditions did not alter the local variations in literacy which had existed among the migrants. There was no wilderness force powerful enough to reduce or locally to disrupt the orderly transmission of literacy. Accordingly there was no "frenzied" educational response which might radically have raised literacy and altered its original variations. In this perspective the motives behind the famous New England school laws should be reassessed. The preface to the major statute expresses concern that "learning may be buried in the graves of our forefathers in Church and Commonwealth." A previous interpretation suggested that this "flowed from the fear of imminent loss of cultural standards, of the possibility that civilization itself would be buried." According to this view "the Puritans quite deliberately transferred the [wilderness-]maimed functions of the family to formal instructional institutions." [78] Possibly, but the family was in fact not maimed and wills show no parallel private frenzy of concern for education. And the entire preface to the law reads:

> It being one chief project of that old deluder, Satan, to keep men from the knowledge of the Scriptures, as in former times keeping them in an unknown tongue, so in these later times by persuading them from the use of tongues, that so at least the true sense and meaning of the original might be clouded with false glosses of Saint-seeming-deceivers; and that learning may not be buried in the graves of our fore-fathers in Church and Commonwealth, the Lord assisting our indeavours; . . . .

There is no reference here to the raw environment or to the family, and the text reads as an English school law would have read had the reforming faction of Puritans had full access to an undistracted Parliament during the Civil War. As Samuel Eliot Morison once observed, "emigration enabled [the Puritans] to carry out in education, as in religion, the system that they thought best." [79]

Nonetheless the question arises why "merely" Puritan school laws were not at first more effective in raising the level of literacy in New England. The laws arose from a traditional Puritan motive which was instrumental in raising literacy in England and which in this compulsory form should have been a most powerful force for education. Yet the generation educated circa 1660 and dying around 1710 showed a literacy little above that of the migrants.[80] Literacy did not even rise enough to perturb or erase the local variations which arose at the time of the migration. Even though they did not arise from a galvanizing fear of the wilderness, the Puritan school laws should have had more impact than this.

Indeed, such improvement in literacy as there was may

not have derived from the public schools. The schools somewhat discriminated against women yet women's literacy rose as fast as men's (Graph 6). New Hampshire was not under the school law yet its literacy rose apace.[81] The same seems to be true of Virginia in this period.[82] Moderate progress around the middle of the literacy spectrum evidently did not require publicly-supported schools in any of these instances, which leads to the suspicion that the mild initial increase in male literacy in New England might also have arisen from sources other than the public schools. Slight improvements in home education or cooperative local pre-schools could nicely explain the gentle rise in both male and female literacy in New England. So, in part, might a small but increasingly literate migration into Suffolk, Fairfield, and Middlesex—counties which account for the bulk of the rise and which seem to have received disproportionately large shares of immigration after 1660.

In a sense the environment may have been to blame for the initial ineffectiveness of the Puritan school laws. Analysis of the period between 1710 and 1760 indicates that the real rise in literacy came only when a more concentrated population enhanced the effectiveness of the schools (see below). This implies that at first the sheer dispersal of the population retarded the impact of the school laws. In this exact sense, then, the raw environment seems to have posed a handicap to education. While neither the threat nor the spur actually described, the environment did prevent the Puritans' laws from taking full effect, delaying the fruits of that Old World impulse to which it had given such scope. This delay, ironically, made possible the orderly transmission of the migrants' original variations in literacy. Had the Puritan school laws been instantly effective in raising literacy those variations might have been eliminated in some areas and exaggerated in others.

THUS a traditional concern for education written into law but somewhat hamstrung by a dispersed population may explain why variations in the migrants' literacy and indeed their actual level of literacy were transmitted largely intact to the third generation. A further consequence of the stalemate was the fact that the traditional forces which had determined personal literacy among the migrants continued to be the determinants of personal literacy for the American generation educated thereafter and dying early in the eighteenth century.

Among both groups, 1660 and 1710, sex was one of the most powerful determinants of literacy. It operated quite independently of all considerations of wealth, occupation, or place of residence, since controlling for these other influences causes virtually no reduction in the relationship between sex and literacy. As mentioned, women were discriminated against as women while men of equal poverty living in the same areas, etc., had greater access to literacy simply because they were men. There may have been a slight reduction in this discrimination in the late seventeenth century, perhaps because home education offered more equal opportunities to women, but this did not entirely erase the heritage of discrimination bequeathed by the migrants.[83]

For men of both periods wealth and occupation were strongly associated with literacy, as is seen in Graphs 9 and 10. Within certain wealth ranges, among certain occupations, wealth and occupation so powerfully determined literacy and literacy so determined wealth and occupation that each step up the ladder of wealth and occupation entailed a much higher probability of literacy. Each of these variables had an independent influence, as has been observed,[84] and together they account for nearly all the variation in literacy explained by the variables available for the male sample.[85]

The correlation of wealth and occupation with literacy was not entirely causal, since there can be little doubt that literacy also led to greater wealth and to certain occupations. Indeed these three variables are so interwoven with one another as to be impenetrable to further analysis. For example, a father's wealth and occupation helped a son

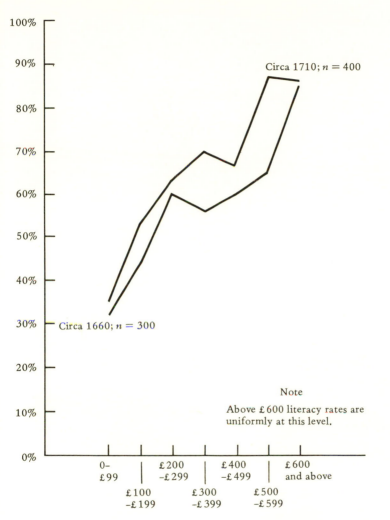

Graph 9: The association of wealth with signatures among men, circa 1660 v. circa 1710

Circa 1710; $n = 400$

Circa 1660; $n = 300$

Note

Above £600 literacy rates are uniformly at this level.

0–
£99

£100
–£199

£200
–£299

£300
–£399

£400
–£499

£500
–£599

£600
and above

Graph 10: The association of occupation with signatures
among men, circa 1660 v. circa 1710

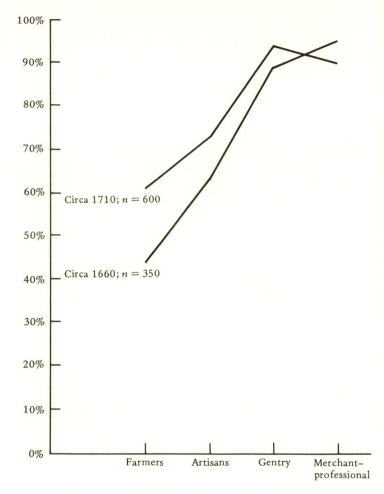

Circa 1710; $n = 600$

Circa 1660; $n = 350$

achieve literacy and simultaneously bequeathed him a certain amount of wealth and perhaps even of occupational skill, and this literacy along with this wealth and this skill determined the son's final wealth and occupation. Economists have long since given up trying to sort out the exact relationships between education, wealth, and occupation.[86] All that can be said is that a certain part of the relationship between these variables must consist of various causal impacts of wealth and occupation in determining literacy.

For what it is worth, an elementary analysis indicates that literacy had more to do with access to occupation and so to wealth than wealth had to do with causing individual literacy.[87] Further, to the extent that literacy determined wealth, rather than wealth literacy, the strength of the relationship between wealth and literacy should vary depending on the relevance of literacy to gaining wealth within the various occupations. This can be tested by studying the relationship of literacy to wealth among farmers and non-farmers. Since most farmers were not deeply involved in commercial transactions, but rather lived a semi-subsistence existence and placed less than half of their output into the market, the majority of which was traded locally, one would not expect there to be much relationship between literacy and wealth among farmers if indeed the primary direction of causation was from literacy to wealth. On the other hand more mercantile types, among whom literacy could make a substantial difference in profits, should show a substantially higher correlation of literacy with wealth. This is exactly the case. The partial correlation for literacy and wealth among farmers (i.e., controlling for other variables) is on the order of .100, whereas the partial correlation for literacy and wealth among non-farmers is over .300. The suggestion is that within the sample wealth was more a product than a pre-condition of literacy. But the data here are biased to this conclusion, since the wealth measured is wealth at death and is highly subject to the impact of literacy while not terribly relevant to its causation. The wealth relevant to the causation of literacy is the wealth of the father at the time a man was educated in literacy, and this measure might tell quite another tale of causes and effects.

Controlling for variations in sex, wealth, and occupation in the data reveals that county of residence and urban versus rural environment were associated with literacy to a small but significant degree. Clearly those variations in the literacy of the migrant stream which had made one county more literate than another and Boston most literate of all, variations passed on to a later generation, involved more than local variations in the sex, wealth, and occupational structure. There remained in both periods significant and substantially identical differences in the literacy of the various localities and so in the literacy possibilities of the individuals living in different localities.

The cumulative impact of all measured variables is such that some 25% of the variation in interpersonal literacy in the samples of 1660 and of 1710 can be associated with sex, wealth, occupation, and location.[88] The relationships are only slightly weaker in 1710 than among the sample educated in England. In one perspective this is a small proportion, for it appears to leave over 75% of the variation in personal literacy unassociated with the "powerful" variables of sex, wealth, and occupation which presumably dominated the causal matrix of interpersonal literacy in both generations. Who knows what else may have determined personal literacy in these periods or whether these unmeasured forces changed drastically between the migrant generation and that educated in America? On the other hand some of the 75% variation unexplained may be due to awkward handling of the variables analyzed. Much of the rest is probably attributable to related but unmeasured variables pertaining to father's literacy, wealth, and occupation. These involve causal forces similar to those outlined here and forces which were not likely to have changed under the social circumstances and level of literacy prevailing in earliest New England. Finally, 25% variation "explained" is not unusually low for analyses of personal variation in educational achievement.[89] For a sample which lived three centuries ago, it is rather satisfying. It at least leaves little doubt that in early New England as in old England, literacy was intimately connected with sex, wealth, and occupation, and that to an appreciable degree such forces determined literacy. This situation was to change drastically in the years leading up to the American Revolution, as new causal forces made virtually all men literate.

WHAT were these new causal forces? Between 1710 and 1760 the rate of increase in male literacy not associated with rising wealth, etc., in the sample was three times as great as before (Graph 1). Despite the inherent obstacles to the spread of literacy at high levels, the rise carried to the very doorstep of universal literacy. What accomplished this transformation?

It is best to begin with the schools and proceed thence to society. It may appear strange to begin with the schools, in view of the evidence of their relative ineffectuality in the preceding period, yet the raw evidence points to the schools as the locus of that expansion of education which accounts for the rise in literacy in eighteenth-century New England. Consider the anatomy of the rise. In the first half of the eighteenth century male literacy increased while female literacy did not rise measurably. The New England public schools are the only mechanism known to discriminate against women.[90] The conclusion is that male literacy rose because ever more men were educated to the required extent by the public schools while such schooling remained largely unavailable to women. Since the rise in literacy was rural, the rural schools were the particular scene of progress, though this is perhaps obvious since nearly all the population and nearly all public schools were located outside the few urban centers.

Confirmation of the schools' role comes from evidence that no eighteenth-century society surpassed 75% male literacy without in some broad way compelling either schooling or support of schools or both.[91] The implication is that formal public action was everywhere an ingredient in the rise of literacy above this level. It can therefore be assumed that the public schools were instrumental in raising male literacy toward universality in New England.

Since the generation dying circa 1760 was educated shortly after 1700, it is not likely that the later efflorescence of private schooling had much role in the literacy of this generation. The most that can be said is that by the middle of the eighteenth century the early development of private elementary education for women may have raised the proportion of adult women who could read a little but could not sign their names, and that by the end of the century later development of this less discriminatory form of education may have increased the proportion of women who could sign. But this is another and a contingent tale.

As for home education, a model in which females alone educated the children cannot account for a rise in male literacy on the order of 60% to 80% within a generation and a half in farm areas where female literacy remained below one-third. Very substantial male participation as home educators would be required. Whether male or female, the home educators would have to refuse to educate a large majority of their daughters to the point of signature while educating the overwhelming proportion of their sons to this extent. These are stringent conditions. In view of previous evidence that a rise in male literacy alone can be accounted for by the public schools and that broad public action was an ingredient wherever a rise to such a high level was found, it seems better to assume that the rise in male literacy was a product of the public schools.[92]

In the seventeenth century the school laws had not been very effective, even when stiffened by Puritan resolve. Literacy had not risen much above the middling level at which it had begun. Now, early in the eighteenth century, something must have happened to make schooling more available or the need for schooling more evident or both. That "something" was pervasive since it reached even the meanest and most distant of farmers and rural artisans and put them in school and so made them literate.

What social forces now brought men and schools together to make men literate? The simplest approach is to ask which variables correlate most closely with the various changes in and conformations of literacy in the eighteenth century. These may tell what was leading simultaneously to schooling and to literacy.[93]

Evidently the cause was not that ever more fathers had enough wealth to educate their sons or because more fathers were in non-farm occupations and hence could see the need to educate their sons. There was some shift to higher wealth and to non-farm occupations in this period, but the rise in literacy was statistically independent of the increases in wealth and in high-literacy occupations, since controlling out these changes does essentially nothing to reduce the rise in literacy.[94] In fact most of the latter-day rise in literacy simply took place among farmers irrespective of any increases of wealth within this group and obviously without new occupational status playing a causal role.[95] (The independence of rising literacy from any social mobility also establishes that for most men the attainment of literacy brought neither increased wealth nor higher occupation.)

Yet the discovery of statistical independence does not rule out all causal relationships between the upward movement of wealth and occupation and the improvement in literacy. It is possible, for example, that the shift to higher wealth and to high-literacy occupations indicated across this period evoked an accelerating increase in literacy because men in less literate ranks wished to equip their sons to take advantage of the apparent opportunity. Most farmers' sons would be educated so as to grasp at a prospect of higher status; few if any would succeed, but the rest would become literate farmers, raising the literacy of this large group. In this way a small increase in social mobility could have evoked a considerable increase in literacy. Yet such an increase would be statistically independent of mobility since it was not personal increase in wealth or in occupational status which led fathers to educate their sons, nor did the sons' literacy generally gain them higher wealth or occupation.

One problem is that the greatest rise in non-farm occupations seems already to have taken place between 1660 and 1710. The majority of the widely literate 1760 males were educated thereafter in a society whose occupational distribution was no longer rising away from but rather moving somewhat back toward farming. It appears unlikely that occupational opportunity evoked the major rise in literacy, unless, that is, one assumes that the crucial experience was that of the fathers of the 1760 sample. These men had grown to maturity while non-farm occupations were proliferating, and may have equipped their sons to meet rising occupational opportunities which in fact no longer existed. The shift to higher wealth presents a more plausible picture. The percentage of the sample worth more than £500 rose from 22% in 1660 to 27% in 1710 and to 40% in 1760. The apparent opportunity to achieve higher wealth could have evoked the widening increase in literacy in the sample.

A greater problem is that Hartford and Middlesex Counties evince the usual rise in literacy without any detectable improvements in the distribution of wealth or of occupations which might have produced or evoked this increase in literacy. These counties include a third of the total sample and are the only ones where the data indicate substantially no upward mobility. The rise in literacy here argues that increased literacy was not a result direct or indirect of net upward property or occupational mobility. Until further evidence is in, other reasons for increased schooling must be sought.

At first it also appears that the forces which were sending men to school and so making them literate were independent not only of positive shifts in the distribution of wealth and occupation, but of all forces represented by wealth and occupation. A sample normalized so as to show no change in its distribution of wealth or of occupation has been analyzed by multiple-regression techniques.[96] In each subsequent period and above all in period III the partial correlation coefficients of wealth and of occupation with literacy decline. By period III these correlations are comparatively negligible.[97] Neither wealth nor occupation any longer correlates to any great degree with interpersonal variations in literacy. At the same time unmeasured forces uniquely strong in period III, represented by a dummy variable called T_3, correlate fairly strongly with interpersonal variations in literacy.[98] It appears that by 1760 new causal forces unrelated to wealth and occupation had emerged to explain interpersonal variations in literacy and presumably these were the forces behind the rise in literacy.

Yet these forces were *not* necessarily unrelated to wealth and to occupation. All that happened is that for reasons which remain to be explained men of nearly all wealth levels and nearly all occupations approached universal literacy, thus ending the high correlation of interpersonal variations in wealth and in occupation with interpersonal variations in literacy by reducing the range of variation in literacy. This does not mean that the forces which raised literacy and thereby made most men literate irrespective of their particular level of wealth or of occupation, forces represented by T_3, had nothing to do with wealth or with occupation. For example, it is perfectly possible that as the eighteenth century wore on, literacy became increasingly necessary to maintaining an estate over £100 or to holding any occupation other than laborer or farmer. Since these categories embraced well over 80% of the male population, it could be that a growing need for literacy in these levels of economic life evoked nearly universal literacy by persuading the mass of men in these categories to educate all their sons in literacy. The result would be to reduce the correlation of interpersonal variations in wealth and occupation with similar variations in literacy since across the broadest range of economic categories all men would now be literate. But it could hardly be said that wealth and occupation had nothing to do with the rise in literacy or with why one man was literate while another was not. Lacking evidence which would prove or disprove conclusively this sort of evocative relationship between wealth, occupation, and literacy, the possibility must be left open that economic forces in this way played a role in the rise in literacy, a possibility which will be added to the causal hypothesis offered here in due course.

Open possibilities do not an hypothesis make, however, and the question is what *does* correlate with literacy and so suggest the forces which made the schools effective. For the moment the only answer is that some very tenuous patterns in the data suggest that crossing a low threshold of population concentration had something to do with the rise in literacy. While it seems unlikely if not impossible that increased wealth was a part of this causal mechanism, nothing is certain, and economic forces of some sort most certainly could have been involved. Let me spell out the hints in the data, then frame an hypothesis around the assumption that "social concentration" led to the rise in literacy by putting men in school.

As of 1760 the variations in local literacy no longer correlated very highly with the original variations in the migrants' literacies.[99] (See Graph 2.) Somehow the original stepladder of migrant literacies, which for a time had reproduced itself among their descendants, had finally been disordered. Or rather local literacy had arranged itself into a new order. The new rank-order of local literacies in 1760 correlates closely with the rank-order of social concentration in these localities at this time. "Social concentration" is here defined as the percentage of the population living in towns with more than a thousand inhabitants.[100]

An example may suggest the processes which could have led to this correlation of local literacies with social concentration. In 1660 Middlesex County had ranked in a tie for third place in literacy, a place it again occupied in 1710. Essex County had been in a tie for fifth place in 1660 and for sixth in 1710. Yet as of 1760 Middlesex ranked sixth while Essex was in a three-way tie for first place with a literacy rate significantly above that in Middlesex. Why the reversal? The counties adjoined and both enjoyed the benefits of school laws and were equidistant from Boston. The answer may lie in the fact that while in the seventeenth century these counties had begun with equally negligible proportions of their populations living in towns larger than several hundred, and in this circumstance the legacy of Middlesex's more literate progenitors had prevailed for a generation or two, by the early eighteenth century Essex was evolving so that a significantly larger proportion of its population lived in towns over this size. By 1710 Essex may have surpassed Middlesex in the proportion of its population living in towns larger than, say, 500 and achieved an absolute proportion living in such towns on the order of 75% as against 50% for Middlesex. Unfortunately no reliable data exist to check this guess, and by 1760 nearly everyone in both counties was living in towns with over 500 inhabitants, so 1760 data cannot repeat 1710 realities. Yet the fact that in 1760 90% of the Essex population lived in towns larger than 1000 as against 50% in Middlesex is most suggestive of real differences which may have begun to prevail as early as 1710 at a lower level of social concentration.[101] For all areas the correlation between variations in 1760 social concentration and variations in 1760 literacy may similarly indicate that emerging differences at a lower level of social concentration had earlier affected the literacy of that generation educated after 1710 in such a way as to impose a new order of local literacies within that generation.[102]

The suggestion is that as early as 1710 emerging variations in "social concentration" had begun to alter inherited variations in local literacy by giving some localities new advantages over others. Could this also imply that a general increase in social concentration throughout New England had something to do with the general rise in literacy? Possibly. It is interesting that the proportion of New England's population living in towns larger than several hundred inhabitants grew faster after 1710, and ultimately included nearly the whole population, just as did literacy.[103]

It may also be significant that two of the three counties which rose from the dispersal of settlement days to the very top on the index of social concentration in 1760, to wit Essex and Fairfield, showed respectively the fastest and third fastest rates of increase in literacy over the long run. Their rapid rates of increase in literacy cannot be ascribed merely to the fact that they had farther to go, since these counties' initial literacy was only a point or two below the average.[104] The other county to reach the top in social concentration, Hartford, began with a literacy ten points above the average so here there was no statistical possibility for a great increase in social concentration to create a rapid rise in literacy. The implication is that in general a rapid rise in social concentration entailed a rapid rise in literacy except where literacy was already unusually high. This is consistent with the idea that a general rise in social concentration was everywhere raising the level of literacy.

If social concentration had an impact it must have come at a very low level. As late as 1760 Middlesex County had little over half of its population living in towns over 1000, and it must have had about this proportion living in towns over perhaps 500 back in 1710. Yet the sample educated circa 1710 and dying in 1760 was over 80% literate. If that was all the base of "concentration" required to reach such wide literacy, then "social concentration" involved little more than evolving out of the extreme dispersal of the settlement years. This was required before literacy could soar, but it was a requirement easily met by any but newly settled societies. In this sense the "extra" involved in social concentration was an extra which mature societies could assume. For this reason Puritan school laws or intense Puritanism alone probably sufficed to raise literacy substantially anywhere in Europe. Earliest New England was an exceptional case requiring social concentration in addition to religious fervor because at first its population was freakishly dispersed.

Such a low threshold would also explain the convergence of local literacy rates in eighteenth-century New England. All localities rapidly crossed the level of concentration required to give the schools maximum effect, so all soon converged at a high level of literacy—except for New Hampshire with its laggard school laws (Graph 2). The low level at which population concentration worked can be dramatized by comparing the countryside with Boston. By 1760 rural New England had caught up with the level of literacy prevailing in Boston even though that city had a far higher and growing level of social concentration. Literacy in Boston had hardly budged as the city rose from a population of 5000 toward one of 15,000, while areas of the countryside where some of the population was still living in towns under 1000 had nonetheless approached Boston in literacy. Truly high concentrations of population were probably counter-productive. As Boston moved into the nineteenth century its literacy may have fallen as a result of an evolving class of poor and illiterate laborers. Whether because commerce bred or attracted illiterates, too much social concentration could actually reduce literacy.[105]

The evidence from Hartford and Middlesex Counties has indicated that increased wealth neither caused nor evoked the rise in literacy, since there was no increase in wealth here but there was the usual rise in literacy. The implication would seem to be that while rising social concentration may have produced increased wealth in some areas, increased wealth was not part of the mechanism by which social concentration produced literacy.[106]

So something labeled "social concentration" appears to be related to emerging differences in literacy and perhaps to the rise in literacy. Since literacy did not cause social concentration, social concentration must have caused literacy. Since the rise in literacy took place in the schools, social concentration must have made schools more effective and/or made the need for schooling more evident, thereby raising literacy. How?

Chiefly it made schooling more available. The school

laws required every town with fifty families, or about 250 persons, to maintain an elementary school. Between the passage of these laws and the early eighteenth century, the proportion of New England's population living in towns smaller than this was at a maximum.[107] The exact proportion is hard to estimate but it could have reached 20%, if towns up to 300 are included on the ground that they could hope to evade the laws. As time passed the population of New England grew, the smaller towns of earliest New England surpassed 300, 400, 500 persons, and of course towns already above this size became still larger. Small new towns constantly emerged, but their proportion of the population was dwarfed by the ever larger mass of the population living in older towns all now well above the size required by the school laws. In Connecticut in 1680 an estimated 17% of the population had lived in towns under 300 persons while by 1708 the proportion was closer to 10% and by 1756 was below 3%. In Massachusetts around 1690 perhaps 15% of the population lived in towns under 300 while by 1765 the proportion was negligible. Most bluntly, then, at first a significant proportion of the population had lived in towns small enough to evade the school law, and after the early eighteenth century that proportion dwindled toward zero.

Increasing town size did more than bring an unschooled minority of the population within the embrace of the law. In all towns it enlarged the tax base, so that the per capita costs of school dwindled. This implied an increased willingness to obey and perhaps to surpass the requirements of the law, since this involved ever less sacrifice to each inhabitant. It also meant that in many towns the additional fees charged local scholars could be reduced. Eventually these fees disappeared, probably because the dwindling per capita costs to taxpayers silenced the demand that the scholars be charged. Schools became essentially free.[108]

Larger towns eventually encountered a problem in making schooling available. Movement of excess population to hamlets several miles from the main village took an ever growing proportion of the inhabitants away from ready access to the schools. The solution was the moving school, which rotated among the various parts of town. Introduced early in the eighteenth century, the moving school quickly became a common feature of town life in New England. There is reason to believe that it brought basic education to the man on the land with greater immediacy than ever before. In the process it enhanced men's awareness of the need for schooling.[109]

Increasing town size made schooling available to all men, then, and ever more cheaply and conveniently. This was true not simply because the entire population came to live in towns larger than 300 persons, but because an ever larger proportion of the population living in towns between, say, 300 and 1000 persons entailed further increases in the availability of education. The correlation of regional variations in literacy with variations in population concentration, and the apparent correlation of both general and local rises in literacy with the rise in population concentration, cannot be accidental. These correlations reveal the pervasive force which made schooling and so literacy universal.

The importance of the availability of schooling is confirmed by an analysis of data from a rural area in early nineteenth-century Sweden. Here, simple proximity to the school seems to have been the most important variable in determining whether or not a child attended school. Father's profession and education were relatively secondary variables in determining attendance.[110] When the school was far from home few children went to school and when it was close to home many children attended. By implication an advance in the availability of schooling such as seems to have occurred in New England could have been quite enough to cause a great increase in school attendance irrespective of other social trends which may or may not have existed.

Still, "population concentration" may have involved more than an increase in the availability of schooling. Concentration may also have led to an increased demand for literacy through the subtle changes which it entailed. In view of the low threshold at which concentration appears to have had a major impact, it is unlikely that it generally en tailed radical changes in the nature of the economy which might have created a tremendous economic demand for literacy. Yet increased concentration might have brought sufficient social diversification, articulation, and specializa tion to alter the dealings of man with man in the direction of written, contractual specificity, making literacy ever more a necessary part of the culture.[111]

Such need did not imply economic progress. Possibly an increase in opportunity evoked an optimistic "need" for literacy in some areas, but in Hartford and Middlesex Counties no such mechanism existed and literacy rose to its peak. It seems more plausible that what enhanced the need for literacy, as indeed for schooling in general, was the necessity of learning to handle new complexities in order to maintain one's position. The very forces which may eventually have led functional literacy's demands to outrun the literacy abilities even of this society could be the very forces which evoked some of the rise in basic literacy in the first place. This is not to say that literacy became an absolute necessity for survival, only that it became increasingly useful to have literacy in order to maintain one's position, whatver its level.[112]

This possibility has already been mentioned. The chief evidence for this tenuous argument is an indication that provisions for education of children in wills became more frequent in the eighteenth century.[113] This is what would be expected if the need for or desire for education were increasing. So would the intensity with which men in the new hamlets fought for access to town schools. As rising wealth and occupational mobility may not have evoked this need, it could have been provoked by structural changes which simply increased the necessity for education. The main evidence against the argument is the continuing massive preponderance of religious books in the inventories of the estates in the sample. The flood of "how-to" book expected to accompany an increase in the need for literacy simply does not materialize, and the focus of literacy emains essentially religious.[114]

Whether it worked by increasing the availability of schooling or also the need for it, social concentration did not require Puritan school laws to work *some* degree of improvement in literacy. Literacy rose steadily in New Hampshire even though school laws there were late and weak.[115] Yet school laws there eventually were, even here, so it is only possible to speculate on what impact social concentration would have had entirely without such statutes. Evidence from New Hampshire and elsewhere indicates that social concentration alone could not move a society to universal male literacy.

At any rate New England grew out of dispersal and literacy spread without limit. The result was to erase the impact of the causal forces which had long determined that one man would be literate and another not. Nearly all men went to school, so nearly all became literate, regardless of their wealth or occupation or of their fathers' status (Graph 11),[116] while only for the minority of illiterates,[117] and for women,[118] were the old bases of selectivity still valid. Puritanism had finally made schools available to men regardless of their station in life, with a little help from social concentration but without any evident assistance from increasing social mobility or other extreme dynamisms in the society.[119] Availability was perhaps all the religion had ever intended and from the evidence it is all it here achieved.

THE analysis confirms the claim that New England was altogether a different social world from that in which unique frenzies and powerful social mobilities both raise literacy to universality and alter its meaning. This was essentially the world of the past, in which a form of Protestantism was the sole force sufficient to generate any high-level change in literacy. The role of "social concentration" in all of this is no more than a minor amendment to the hypothesis proposed by Michael Sanderson, that prior to

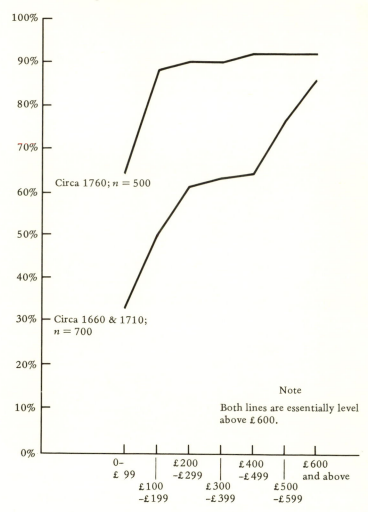

Graph 11: The association of wealth with signatures among men, circa 1660 & 1710 v. circa 1760

Circa 1760; $n = 500$

Circa 1660 & 1710;
$n = 700$

Note

Both lines are essentially level above £600.

the mid-nineteenth century the Protestant religion and its associated schools were the prime forces involved in raising literacy, while the enticements or demands of economic and social change had little impact. The data here strongly support this thesis with the emandation that in New England the population was so dispersed and the economy so subsistence-oriented that a modicum of social concentration and perhaps a minimum of structural economic development were required to make the Protestant school laws effective.[120] And of course Protestantism's effectiveness was limited largely to the extent of male literacy.

II

New England Literacy in Comparative Perspective

✠

I<small>F</small> then there was no "American" social dynamic at work in New England, but only the impact of Puritan ideology augmented by social concentration, what was the course of literacy elsewhere in America? If there was no frenzied reaction to the wilderness in New England, it is doubtful that such a reaction spurred literacy elsewhere. If existing social mobility was not instrumental in raising literacy in New England, then it is not likely that any social mobility boosted literacy to high levels elsewhere. The lesson of New England is that the Protestant impulse, coalesced into some form of broad legal compulsion toward or into the wide availability of education, was the crucial source of universal male literacy in this world of the past. Since the other colonies did not evince this singular Protestant impulse, male literacy elsewhere in America may not have risen to anything like universality.

Lower literacy elsewhere in the colonies would mean that a substantial minority of men would be ineligible for the benefits of whatever educational ethos did exist. The association of social status with literacy would probably endure in these areas. In addition, there is little reason to expect that literacy here entailed "new" attitudes any more than in New England. Women's literacy should have performed elsewhere more or less as it did in New England, rising indifferently from a low to a less low level. These predictions do not fit theories which imply a male literacy rising toward universality throughout eighteenth-century America, and a literacy widely involved with "liberated" attitudes.[121] Nonetheless the description is consistent with the evidence of New England, that this was a world of fewer and lesser social forces than has been thought, in which without intense Protestantism literacy's changes were slow or virtually nonexistent.

Evidence from colonial Pennsylvania and Virginia largely confirms these predictions. Male literacy rose to the two-thirds level by the early eighteenth century, then stagnated there for the rest of the colonial era. One-third of men were left effectively outside the educational system. In Virginia the statistical correlation between social status and literacy remained as high as it had been in the seventeenth century. There is evidence that here the charitable attitudes of literates remained as traditional as those of illiterates. The data on women's literacy is weak but the combined information from Pennsylvania and Virginia indicates only the same tentative rise as prevailed in New England. In all respects this is a literacy environment very like that in eighteenth-century England. It is the environment of pre-industrial English and American society in the absence of intense Protestantism.

The primary source of literacy data for the rest of the colonies are some three thousand wills from Pennsylvania and Virginia. The data from Pennsylvania have been presented by Alan Tully.[122] Extensive data for Virginia have been analyzed in more detail by the author. The Virginia wills are supplemented by the well-known investigations of P.A. Bruce, which include data from other sources which are essentially consistent with the results obtained from wills.[123]

MALE literacy seems to have risen to a substantial level in all American colonies by the beginning of the eighteenth century. The raw data from Chester and Lancaster Counties in Pennsylvania show a male literacy of 70% for the generation dying in the 1730s. A comparable projection for New England at this time would be around 75%. Adjustments for the biases of age, wealth, and occupation would bring these figures closer to 65% and 70%, respectively, but the fact remains that early in the eighteenth century the male population of Pennsylvania appears to have enjoyed a literacy rate within five points of the rate of New England. The same is true of Virginia, where the generation dying 1705-15 had shown an unadjusted signature rate of 67%, which would correspond to a rate of 62% for a more representative sample of that cohort, a rate only a little more than five points below the rate of the similarly adjusted projection for New England (see Graph 12).[124] Nearly two-thirds of men throughout America were literate.

What enabled these other colonies to keep up? They lacked New England's intense Puritanism and the school laws it created, yet kept pace with the northern colonies for several decades into the eighteenth century. The reason may be twofold. In the first place the evidence is that New England's school laws were not yet as effective as they would later become, so the pace set by the Puritan colonies was not rapid. Meanwhile, the stream of transatlantic migration, which was flowing into the other colonies, seems to have contained an ever higher proportion of literate men. For example, Dutch men arriving in New York around the middle of the seventeenth century had a 75% signature rate whereas men arriving around the turn of the eighteenth century averaged over 85% signatures.[125] In Pennsylvania German males arriving in the 1720s showed a 73% rate, while nearly 80% of later arrivals made signatures.[126] Even earlier, a 45% signature rate for men leaving wills in Virginia before 1650 was surpassed by a broader sample weighted toward more recent arrivals, signing the Loyalty Oath of 1652.[127] Men leaving wills between 1670 and 1680 also evinced a higher signature rate than that of the pre-1650 sample; these later will-leavers were essentially contemporaneous with the group signing the 1652 Oath, and they too were heavily weighted toward post-1650 ar-

rivals.[128] Everywhere the trend was toward a stream of
male migrants whose literacy rose from the halfway mark
early in the seventeenth century to around three-quarters by
the turn of the eighteenth. Thus as migration to New England tapered off and the school laws moved literacy slowly
through its mid-range, the other colonies received an increasingly literate migration which raised their literacy also
through the middle of the spectrum. The result was a uniform rate of male literacy throughout early eighteenth-
century America.

Alternate explanations are possible, but must deal with
the evidence of migration. It is quite possible that when literacy is in the 30-70% range a mixture of scattered public
and private schools with home education suffices to raise
literacy modestly. This mixture could explain the rise in
literacy in seventeenth-century Pennsylvania and Virgina.
Yet the role of such a form of indigenous education must
be placed in the perspective of a massive migration which
meant that most men living in the middle and southern
colonies in the seventeenth century and dying early in the
eighteenth were migrants. The evidence is that the literacy
of these migrants rose with each succeeding wave, hence
it is doubtful that informal or non-public schooling explains
much of the rising movement of literacy in the rest of
seventeenth-century America.

Thus the causal context explaining the growth of male
literacy in seventeenth-century Pennsylvania and Virginia:
their progress relative to New England is explained in part
by the fact that northern literacy was not yet improving
at its maximum rate; their equivalent advance did not stem
from any evident fear of the wilderness,[129] and, while mild
indigenous educational efforts might easily explain such
modest progress in the middle of the spectrum, more stress
might be put on massive and increasingly literate in-migration. Migration itself is a force as much traditional as radical. It radically selects for literate men from the societies
of origin, yet those men are still the products of a traditional European context.

Whatever its origins, the moderate advance of male lit-

LIBRARY OF MOUNT ST. MARY'S COLLEGE EMMITSBURG, MARYLAND

eracy to the two-thirds level left intact the traditional forces which determined who was literate and who was not. Similarly literacy continued to open doors which illiteracy did not. As a result interpersonal variations in male literacy in these "other" colonies were intimately associated with wealth and occupation. As in New England at this time, the rich were almost entirely literate, while only half of the farmers and a third of the poor of whatever occupation were literate (Graphs 14, 16). This association may in turn have reinforced ancient social distinctions. And, as will be seen in Table 6, even more than in early eighteenth-century New England literacy did not appear to entail new attitudes, which is hardly surprising since many of these colonists elsewhere were educated in Europe.

THE rest of the eighteenth century is the test of literacy elsewhere in colonial America. Indications are that literacy failed to rise from the level it had reached early in the century. From the generations educated after the middle of the seventeenth century and dying in the first half of the eighteenth at least up to the generation educated just prior to the middle of the eighteenth century and dying shortly before the nineteenth, male literacy remained at the two-thirds mark (Graph 12).

In Chester and Lancaster Counties in Pennsylvania, the aggregate unadjusted signature rate for males did not move from a level just above two-thirds. Inertia was as characteristic of Chester County, which began the century a trifle below 75% and ended it at the same point, as of Lancaster County, where the rate began and ended just below 65%. A mild uptrend in Chester County wills circa 1760-70 was not continued with sufficient strength to raise the aggregate level. Within both counties, German and non-German populations showed roughly similar rates, and while the former improved their literacy somewhat it was not enough to raise the aggregate level of these counties above what it had been earlier in the century.[130]

The same appears to be true of male literacy in eighteenth-century Virginia. For all statistical purposes the male signature rate remained at two-thirds right up to the generation dying in the 1790s. Here also there were local increases which may be significant and will be discussed later, yet three of the seven counties sampled showed no change while a fourth shows an uptrend of only marginal significance.[131] The stagnation of literacy in Virginia can be seen in Graph 12 but is better summed up in the following table:

Table 4

	1705–62	1762–97
Males: signatures	66%	68%
Males: marks	34%	32%
	n=437	n=648

The rate for 1796-97 alone was exactly 67%, as it had been in the first decades of the century.

While New England wills approached a rate of 90% male literacy, wills in colonies elsewhere remained near the 67% level which all colonies had once occupied. Adjusting these raw data for their small net upward biases would place New England male literacy in the 1790s closer to 85% and that of Pennsylvania and Virginia closer to 60%.[132] In New England at this time no more than 15% of men were unable to sign their names. Perhaps half of these may have attended the public schools long enough to learn to read. Some of the remainder represented the hard-core of uneducable persons which plagues any society. In the end it could be that only 5% of New England men were ablebodied illiterates. Elsewhere as many as 40% of men made marks. Without a public school system to expose boys at least to reading, the proportion of total illiterates among these markers must have been substantially higher than in

New England. Even with the uneducable removed, it is possible that 25% of men outside New England were able-bodied but quite illiterate.

The enduring reality of mass illiteracy can be dramatized by a look at the middle and lower strata of society in Virginia. In New England men worth less than £600 had approached the 90% literacy level by 1790. In Virginia men worth less than £200 in personal estate, equivalent to less than £600 total estate, showed a signature rate of 55% throughout the eighteenth century (Graph 13). Net downward adjustments for the pro-literacy biases of occupation and selectivity in the sample would suggest a signature rate closer to 50% for men in these commonest categories of wealth. It appears possible that even toward the end of the eighteenth century half the middle and lower class males in Virginia were unable to sign their names. With readers and incompetents deducted, able-bodied but total illiterates could have constituted fully one-third of these ordinary levels of male society.

To dramatize the level of literacy outside New England in still another way, as of the 1790s not one county among those measured in Pennsylvania and Virginia had surpassed the 75% male signature rate which New Hampshire had long since reached. At the end of the eighteenth century prosperous Chester County, distinguished Westmoreland, and urbanizing Richmond had no more than equalled the literacy achieved a generation before by New England's least literate area. It seems clear that these other areas of America did not benefit from the crucial causal force which moved most of New England into a class by itself.

Those who disagree might suggest that strong and perhaps specifically religious forces were indeed at work raising the level of indigenous literacy in these other colonies, and that a decreasingly literate in-migration counterbalanced such forces, leaving the level of literacy static. Yet the fragments of data available all indicate that the rise in migrant literacy continued through the first half of the eighteenth century. It might be thought that the Scots-Irish

Graph 12: Male signatures on wills: Raw data

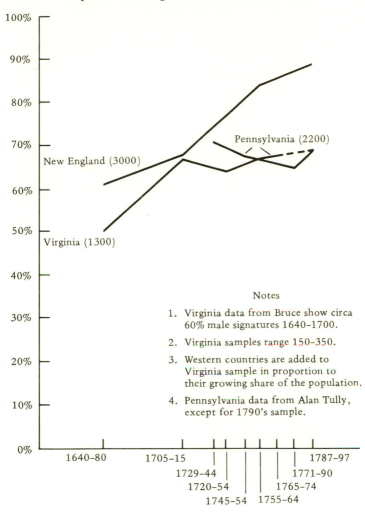

Notes

1. Virginia data from Bruce show circa 60% male signatures 1640-1700.

2. Virginia samples range 150-350.

3. Western countries are added to Virginia sample in proportion to their growing share of the population.

4. Pennsylvania data from Alan Tully, except for 1790's sample.

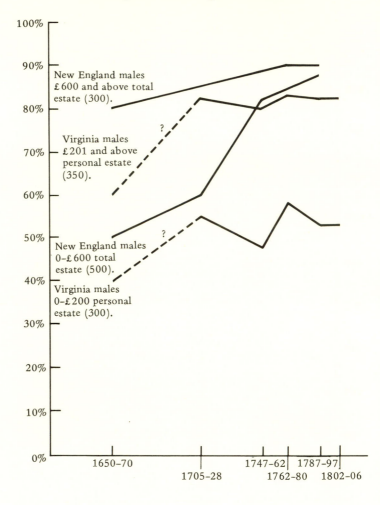

Graph 13: Male signatures by wealth-group in New England and in Virginia over time

New England males
£600 and above total
estate (300).

Virginia males
£201 and above
personal estate
(350).

?

New England males
0–£600 total
estate (500).

Virginia males
0–£200 personal
estate (300).

?

100%

90%

80%

70%

60%

50%

40%

30%

20%

10%

0%

1650–70   1705–28   1747–62   1787–97   1802–06   1762–80

Graph 14: Virginia male signatures by wealth over time

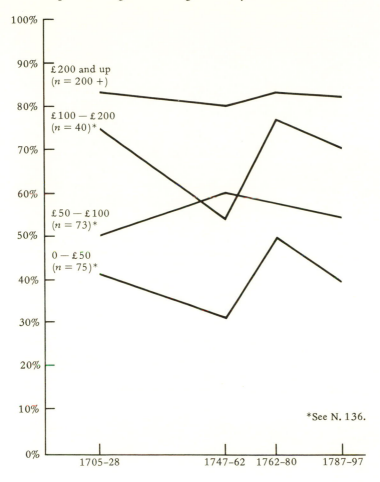

£200 and up
(*n* = 200 +)

£100 — £200
(*n* = 40)*

£50 — £100
(*n* = 73)*

0 — £50
(*n* = 75)*

*See N. 136.

1705–28   1747–62   1762–80   1787–97

would constitute an exception. An influx of heavily illiterate Scots-Irish into Pennsylvania and Virginia could have counterbalanced a rising trend of indigenous literacy, leaving stagnation. There are two problems with this hypothesis. In the first place the Scots-Irish were part of a Presbyterian culture which, in Scotland at least, had achieved a literacy above the 75% level by the mid-eighteenth century.[133] Ulster may not have matched the Scots achievement, but it would be difficult to ascribe massive illiteracy to this radical Protestant society. Second, the evidence so far is that the selectivity inherent in migration could be worth as much as an absolute ten points above the literacy prevailing in the mother country, in this case Ulster. These things considered it is difficult to see how the Scots-Irish influx could have been less than 50% literate and 70% would be a plausible figure. This is confirmed by Tully's analysis of the wills of settlers in Lancaster County. This county was founded in 1729 and a very large proportion of its settlers were recent migrants to America. The wills of German settlers show a literacy rate around 65%, as did the wills of Englishmen, but so did the wills of the Scots-Irish. If this was the literacy level of Scots-Irish migrants, it would not hide a strong tendency of indigenous literacy elsewhere to rise above this level. Yet the aggregate rates for Pennsylvania and Virginia show no such rise.[134]

The suspicion that indigenous literacy was not rising is confirmed by the performance of counties which did not receive a massive Scots-Irish influx. Tidewater Westmoreland and Middlesex remained at essentially the same level:

Table 5

	1705–15	1720–49	1758–62	1771–97
Signatures	72%	69%	68%	74%
Marks	28%	31%	32%	26%
	n=100	n=100	n=100	n=100

Literacy in older areas stagnated somewhat above the level in newer counties for reasons which will be discussed later, but stagnate it did. It is difficult to claim that the Scots-Irish counterbalanced an indigenous, possibly religious impulse toward higher literacy, for there is no evidence of such an indigenous rise.

Something was lacking in these other colonies which was present in New England. Neither social mobility nor social concentration is the missing crucial force since insofar as either existed it was present in all colonies and neither in New England nor quite evidently elsewhere did either of these forces alone raise literacy toward universality. Widespread fear of the wilderness was not present in New England, so it is not the vital element, and if such a fear had existed it would have occurred in other colonies where there is no evidence it had any impact. In simplest terms male literacy in these other areas of eighteenth-century America failed to rise toward universality because these areas lacked intense Protestantism and consequent school laws.

Even the high initial literacy, the religious concern, and the strong communities of the Pennsylvania Germans may not have been enough to match on a small scale the larger New England achievement. Germans dying in Lancaster County 1765-74, presumably including a fair proportion of men raised in Pennsylvania, still showed a literacy rate no higher than two-thirds. What the Germans could not accomplish the English and Scots-Irish did not manage either. Despite massive evidence of charity school movements, laws compelling education of apprentices, and itinerant schoolmasters, male literacy in Pennsylvania and Virginia did not advance substantially during the course of the eighteenth century. The indications are that at this time a uniformly and intensely Protestant society and, above all, the systematic state action which emerges from such a society were essential to moving male literacy the last large step to universality.[135]

WHERE that step was not taken, as in eighteenth-century Virginia and Pennsylvania, the correlation between social status and literacy rates continued to exist. In Virginia the most wealthy men were commonly literate while among the lower orders literacy was nearly the exception (Graph 14).[136] Substantial literacy still entailed a relationship of literacy with social status.

In a society so static that the quantity of literacy remained fixed and its social structure intact, it was not to be expected that literate men increasingly acquired "liberated" attitudes. The Virginia sample indicates that men who became literate always showed the same traditional attitudes as illiterates. Among the Virginia men the low level of charitable concern actually declined, both among literates and illiterates, as it had in New England. For literates as for illiterates, the objects of charitable concern tended even more than in New England to be persons connected with the family, rather than persons not so connected, and tended even more to be persons of whatever ilk instead of abstract causes, while gifts to causes were even more rarely directed outside the home village. This pattern continued right up to the end of the eighteenth century:

Table 6

	GIFTS TO A PERSON WITHIN THE VILLAGE CONNECTED WITH THE FAMILY (SERVANTS).	GIFTS TO A PERSON WITHIN THE VILLAGE NOT CONNECTED WITH THE FAMILY (MINISTERS).	GIFTS TO A CAUSE WITHIN THE VILLAGE (THE POOR, RELIGION, EDUCATION).	GIFTS TO A CAUSE OUTSIDE THE VILLAGE.
Virginia Gifts 1630–80	28 44%	28 44%	6 10%	1 2%
Virginia Gifts 1705–97	32 38%	39 45%	14 16%	1 1%

New England Literacy in Comparative Perspective

Table 7

	GIFTS TO A PERSON WITHIN THE VILLAGE CONNECTED WITH THE FAMILY (SERVANTS).	GIFTS TO A PERSON WITHIN THE VILLAGE NOT CONNECTED WITH THE FAMILY (MINISTERS).	GIFTS TO A CAUSE WITHIN THE VILLAGE (THE POOR, RELIGION, EDUCATION).	GIFTS TO A CAUSE OUTSIDE THE VILLAGE.
Literates' Gifts 1630–1797	35 33%	49 47%	19 18%	2 2%
Illiterates' Gifts 1630–1797	25 55%	18 43%	1 2%	0

Table 8

	GIFTS TO A PERSON WITHIN THE VILLAGE CONNECTED WITH THE FAMILY (SERVANTS).	GIFTS TO A PERSON WITHIN THE VILLAGE NOT CONNECTED WITH THE FAMILY (MINISTERS).	GIFTS TO A CAUSE WITHIN THE VILLAGE (THE POOR, RELIGION, EDUCATION).	GIFTS TO A CAUSE OUTSIDE THE VILLAGE.
Literates' Gifts 1630–80	13 36%	16 44%	6 17%	1 3%
Literates' Gifts 1705–97	22 32%	33 48%	13 19%	1 1%

There is reason to believe that once the greater wealth of literates is controlled out, here as in New England most of the small ongoing differences between literates and illiterates disappear.

To look at the objects of concern in another way, in Vir-

[85]

ginia alms and prayers dominated, leaving even less room than in New England for an impulse toward rehabilitative gifts such as those to education or to municipal betterments. This was true even in the eighteenth century:

Table 9

	GIFTS TO THE POOR	GIFTS TO RELIGION	GIFTS TO EDUCATION	GIFTS TO MUNICIPALITY
Gifts 1630–80	76	8	0	0
	90%	10%		
Gifts 1705–25	51	7	2	0
	85%	12%	3%	
Gifts 1728–97	27	0	0	0
	100%			

In this instance there is absolutely no distinction between the behavior of literates and illiterates. There is no tendency of literates alone to move increasingly toward education or municipal betterments. Among all Virginian givers in all periods, the traditional aims of alleviation and piety remained foremost. What Puritanism could not do in New England, its absence could not accomplish elsewhere. It seems that in most of colonial America neither the quantity nor the quality of literacy was revolutionized by the events of the eighteenth century.

Possibly the quantity or even the quality of literacy outside New England began to change after the period under study. It has been said that America enjoyed a remarkable educational efflorescence in the decades after 1750.[137] This could have led to a substantial increase and/or qualitative alteration in literacy by the generation educated circa 1760, influential in the 1780s and 1790s, and the 1800s, and dying thereafter. Yet data from 250 Virginia wills 1803–6 show only 70% literacy. It is difficult to measure the depth of the skills involved in literacy, and this may have improved, but for what it is worth there is no evidence that pro- longed schooling among literates led to a shift of charitable attitudes toward a wider arena or to rehabilitative pur- poses.[138] Whether or not literacy rose or altered attitudes in the generations educated after 1760, there remains the possibility that the social forces of these times further es- calated the demands on men's understanding and left them relatively less literate than ever before, as may have been happening throughout the early nineteenth-century world.

In any event the literacy of that American generation which took the colonies into the Revolution was less than perfect. It seems probable that one-quarter of the genera- tion born around 1730, educated around 1740, politically influential in the '60s, '70s, and '80s, and dying early in the 1790s, was totally illiterate. Including New England in the total would not much alter the level of enduring illit- eracy since two-thirds of the population lived outside New England. Illiteracy actually prevailed among men of menial wealth and status. In such a context, there is no indication that literacy brought new attitudes to men, whatever their status. The literacy of most Americans up to the first revolutionary generation is best compared in all respects with literacy in contemporaneous England. The fixed quan- tity, hierarchical structure, and traditional attitudinal quali- ties of literacy which Pennsylvania and Virginia suggest were typical of eighteenth-century America are precisely the features of literacy prevailing in England at the time.

In England adult male literacy hovered around 60% throughout the eighteenth century, according to results re- ported by Roger Schofield of the Cambridge Group for the Study of Population and Social Structure.[139] Previous work by Lawrence Stone had indicated that the generation educated in the seventeenth century was closer to 50%

literacy,[140] which might suggest a slow rise to the 60% level which definitely prevailed by 1754, but in any event literacy was above the halfway point early in the eighteenth century and it remained around 60% right up to the generation married around 1815.[141]

How does this compare to America? Very closely, once the data are adjusted to represent the same age cohorts and the biases of the wills are removed. The generation born around 1700, educated in literacy around 1710, married circa 1725, and dying approximately in 1760, shows a raw signature rate of 67% in Pennsylvania and Virginia as compared with a conservative estimate of 50% in England. Feebleness and forgetfulness bias the data from colonial wills downward, but the wealth and occupational selectivities of wills bias the data upward even more, so that a net downward adjustment of five to ten points may be needed to bring the signature rate in wills closer to that of the adult male population. A downward adjustment of seven points has been imposed. This would bring the colonial data down to 60% signatures as against the 50% estimated for the adult male population in England. By comparison the New England men born around 1700 showed a signature rate of nearly 85%, which could not plausibly be moved much below 80% by any adjustments.[142]

By the generation born around 1730, educated in literacy around 1740, marrying circa 1755, and dying after 1790, the adjusted 60% level of colonial literacy outside New England had been equalled by a broad sample of Englishmen of the same approximate age (Graph 15).[143] In this influential generation England enjoyed the same level of literacy as most of colonial America. In both places, at least one man in four was illiterate.[144]

In England as in most of America literacy was naturally still linked to occupation and to wealth. Merchants, gentry, and professionals were above the 90% level, while artisans were closer to 75%, farmers near 50%, and laborers well

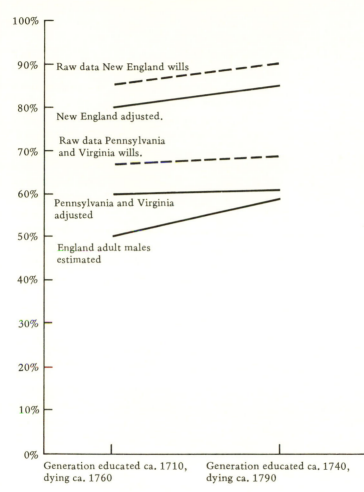

Graph 15: Schematic comparison of male signatures in England and America

100%

90% — Raw data New England wills

80% — New England adjusted.

Raw data Pennsylvania
70% — and Virginia wills.

60% —

Pennsylvania and Virginia
adjusted

50% —

England adult males
estimated

40% —

30% —

20% —

10% —

0% —

Generation educated ca. 1710,
dying ca. 1760

Generation educated ca. 1740,
dying ca. 1790

Graph 16: Male signatures v. wealth in Virginia and in England

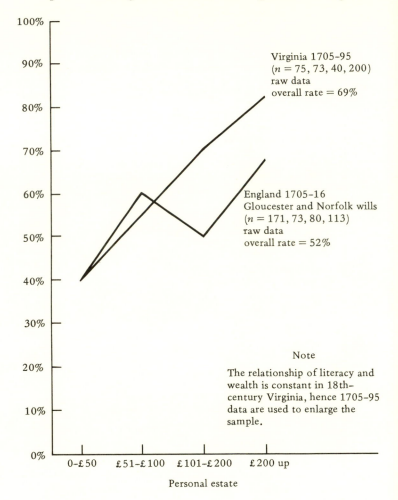

Virginia 1705–95
($n = 75, 73, 40, 200$)
raw data
overall rate = 69%

England 1705–16
Gloucester and Norfolk wills
($n = 171, 73, 80, 113$)
raw data
overall rate = 52%

Note

The relationship of literacy and wealth is constant in 18th–century Virginia, hence 1705–95 data are used to enlarge the sample.

Personal estate

Graph 17: Signatures by occupation:
New England v. England 1700-25

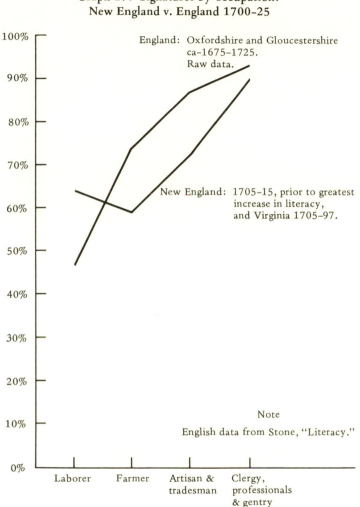

England: Oxfordshire and Gloucestershire
ca–1675–1725.
Raw data.

New England: 1705–15, prior to greatest
increase in literacy,
and Virginia 1705–97.

Note
English data from Stone, "Literacy."

Graph 18: Women's signatures on wills

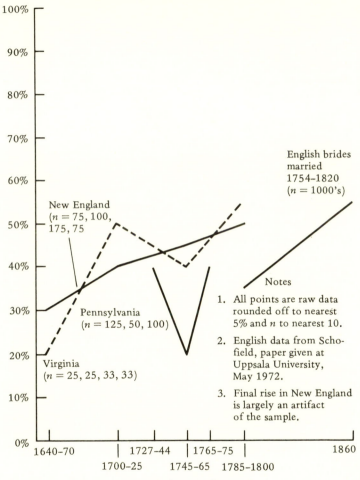

Women dying in the years

[92]

below—rather as in Virginia. Here also, wealth caused, resulted from, and so was intertwined with personal literacy such that the rich were usually literate and the poor most often not—as in Virginia (Graph 16).[145] Only in New England were these differences disappearing, and New England was not the hub of eighteenth-century Anglo-America.

There may have been some interesting transatlantic variations within the traditional causal structure of interpersonal literacy. Early in the eighteenth century, the variation in literacy between occupations may have been much greater in England than in America (Graph 17). If so, this was largely because of the plight of English laborers, who were far behind farmers and stretched downward the range of occupational differences in England. Indeed it is the great mass of laborers not included in the documents who often lower the adjusted overall literacy rate of English samples a little below the adjusted American rate. America did better in its overall literacy because of the absence of a large class of laborers greatly inferior in literacy. Yet the absence of this huge laboring group was not enough to make American literacy vastly higher than the English. The reason may be that, laborers aside, Americans of any given occupation were distinctly less literate than their English counterparts (Graph 17). This points to an irony: leaving the mass of laborers behind brought America a higher overall literacy, but American farmers, artisans, tradesmen, and gentry were less literate than their counterparts in England, so the result was an overall literacy only slightly above that in England. America was progression and regression rolled into one. The progression, however, disappears on considering that if slaves were included in the analysis, not only the level of literacy by occupation, but also the overall level of male literacy, would be lower in America.

To take the theme of regression a bit further, it appears that the relationships between literacy and wealth were more consistently powerful in America than in England

(Graph 16). In early eighteenth-century Virginia the relationship as graphed is nearly perfect across the entire
range of wealth. English data graphed on the same scale
show a much weaker relationship, primarily because there
is no appreciable link between literacy and wealth in the
mid-range of wealth. Evidently the English middle classes
were uniquely free of economic and status interactions associated with literacy. Indeed, if the English line on the
graph were stretched out to the right, as it should be since
pounds sterling were worth more than colonial currencies,
it would appear that throughout the full range of English
society literacy was less involved with wealth than in America.

In short, slaves included, none of America's occupational
groups may have had as high a literacy as similar groups in
England, while within American society wealth and literacy
were perhaps more intensely correlated than in England.
Still, these "regressive" possibilities are only embellishments
of that general correlation between literacy and social distinctions which continued to echo through English and
through most of colonial society during the eighteenth century. The basic quantity and social structure of literacy were
essentially the same in both areas.

English wills show that literate and illiterate testators
maintained traditional charitable attitudes throughout the
eighteenth century, indicating that here as in Virginia
neither society at large nor literacy in particular was incul-
cating increasingly "modern" attitudinal qualities.[146] These
traditional attitudes were of course evidently also sustained in New England. In England, as everywhere, all
testators showed a declining level of charitable involvement. Those who did leave gifts always focused roughly half
of their thoughts on persons rather than on abstract causes
and a large share of these thoughts went to persons linked
to the testator's family. Gifts to causes were almost entirely concentrated within the testator's own village. Consciousness was always strongly directed toward the family,
toward persons, and within the village:

[94]

Table 10

	GIFTS TO A PERSON WITHIN THE VILLAGE CONNECTED WITH THE FAMILY (SERVANTS).	GIFTS TO A PERSON WITHIN THE VILLAGE NOT CONNECTED WITH THE FAMILY (MINISTERS).	GIFTS TO A CAUSE WITHIN THE VILLAGE (THE POOR, RELIGION, EDUCATION).	GIFTS TO A CAUSE OUTSIDE THE VILLAGE.
Gifts 1700–20	53	14	134	8
	25%	7%	64%	4%
Gifts 1755–65	27	22	46	3
	28%	22%	47%	3%

In England, as in Virginia (and in some respects also as in New England), there are hints that literates tended slightly more than illiterates to give outside the family, to abstract causes, and beyond the confines of the village. Within all these locations, gifts outside the village, while rare, appear to be a form of behavior available exclusively to literates. Yet neither here nor elsewhere did such marginal tendencies amount to a massively different attitudinal structure among literates, nor were literates' attitudes becoming more "modern" with time:

Table 11

	GIFTS TO A PERSON WITHIN THE VILLAGE CONNECTED WITH THE FAMILY (SERVANTS).	GIFTS TO A PERSON WITHIN THE VILLAGE NOT CONNECTED WITH THE FAMILY (MINISTERS).	GIFTS TO A CAUSE WITHIN THE VILLAGE (THE POOR, RELIGION, EDUCATION).	GIFTS TO A CAUSE OUTSIDE THE VILLAGE.
Literates' Gifts 1700–65	58	30	136	11
	25%	10%	60%	5%
Illiterates' Gifts 1700–65	22	6	44	0
	31%	8%	61%	

Table 12

	GIFTS TO A PERSON WITHIN THE VILLAGE CONNECTED WITH THE FAMILY (SERVANTS).	GIFTS TO A PERSON WITHIN THE VILLAGE NOT CONNECTED WITH THE FAMILY (MINISTERS).	GIFTS TO A CAUSE WITHIN THE VILLAGE (THE POOR, RELIGION, EDUCATION).	GIFTS TO A CAUSE OUTSIDE THE VILLAGE.
Literates' Gifts 1700–20	39 25%	10 6%	101 64%	8 5%
Literates' Gifts 1755–65	19 25%	20 26%	35 45%	3 4%

In the end, controlling for the greater wealth of literates may reduce their pattern of behavior to one nearly identical to that of illiterates, as appears to happen elsewhere.

English givers shared with their Virginia counterparts a focus on alleviative and pious giving even stronger than that in New England. Giving to rehabilitative purposes was virtually nonexistent at all times:

Table 13

	GIFTS TO THE POOR	GIFTS TO RELIGION	GIFTS TO EDUCATION	GIFTS TO MUNICIPALITY
Gifts 1700–20	232 90%	22 8%	4 2%	0
Gifts 1755–65	109 82%	24 18%	0	0

Within this aggregate there is no difference in the behavior of literates and illiterates, and no tendency of literates to move toward rehabilitative giving as time passed.[147]

Before summing up, the fate of women's literacy offers a final point of transatlantic comparison. Here too, it may not be simply a matter of England resembling Virginia but of all areas around the Atlantic, even New England, being fundamentally similar within a basically traditional world (Graph 18). If the American data were adjusted downward to compensate for the exceptional wealth of women leaving wills, they would indicate essentially the same trend implied by the data from English marriage registers. It is doubtful that in eighteenth-century America women's literacy advanced much if at all, but over the long run women's literacy everywhere in Anglo-America seems to have moved from a rate below 20% early in the seventeenth century toward a rate around 50% in the mid-nineteenth century. In the long run, however, male literacy everywhere outside New England rose at roughly the same rate, and at much higher levels, approaching the three-quarters mark by mid-nineteenth century and universality soon thereafter. Thus, relative to men, women of the early nineteenth century were no better off than their forebears two hundred years earlier.

Beneath New England's burning Protestantism and consequent universal male literacy, Anglo-America was a world in which literacy moved glacially at a middling level. Many men were illiterate and, because of an intimate association of literacy with social status, the majority of men of low status was illiterate. Everywhere the attitudes of men seem to have remained personal, local, palliative. Nowhere was women's literacy raised enough to erase an ancient legacy of discrimination. This profile of literacy unites much of America with England in an eighteenth-century literacy environment best described as static.

THE story, then, is simple and returns full circle to Protestantism. In New England Protestantism was instrumental in whatever major changes took place in literacy. Elsewhere in the Anglo-American world that force did not exist in a form intense enough to generate systematic educational ac-

Graph 19: Schematic comparison of adult male literacy in New England, Scotland, and Sweden

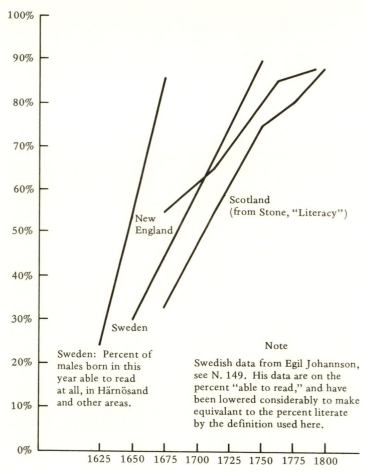

100%

90%

80%

70%

60%

Scotland
(from Stone, "Literacy")

New
England

50%

40%

30%

Sweden

Note

Sweden: Percent of
males born in this
year able to read
at all, in Härnösand
and other areas.

20%

Swedish data from Egil Johannson,
see N. 149. His data are on the
percent "able to read," and have
been lowered considerably to make
equivalant to the percent literate
by the definition used here.

10%

0%

1625 1650 1675 1700 1725 1750 1775 1800

tion and the muted social forces of the day probably did not significantly alter any feature of literacy.

A look at the rest of the Atlantic world dramatizes the salient role of Protestantism. In all this world the only areas to show a rapid rise in literacy to levels approaching universality were small societies whose intense Protestantism led them widely to offer or to compel in some way the education of their people. In Calvinist Scotland, a system of compulsory elementary education appears to have raised adult male literacy from 33% around 1675 to nearly 90% by 1800, a pace surpassing the rate of improvement in male literacy in New England. As a result Scotland reached the threshold of universal male literacy simultaneously with New England.[148] Sweden provides a more dramatic example of the power of Protestant concern. Graph 19 presents a schematic version of the growth of literacy in this nation. It indicates that both men *and women* had achieved nearly universal literacy, as literacy is defined in this study, before the middle of the eighteenth century. The pace may have been faster still: in the parishes of Härnösand diocese, far to the north, the proportion of males "able to read" rose from 50% to 98% in the period 1645–1714.[149] If this pace held throughout Sweden, it would be the only example of a pre-modern rate of growth in literacy which can match twentieth-century achievements.[150]

At the same time, Sweden reaffirms the traditional nature of the forces at work. The impulse came from the Protestant State Church, whose catechetical examinations of the populace included rigorous tests of literacy administered almost annually to every man, woman, and child by the local pastor. The Church's influence was so pervasive and the practice of periodic examination so compelling that no formal law requiring school support or attendance was needed to universalize literacy. Pastoral examinations, ministerial tutoring, and home education achieved a revolution in basic education entirely within the aegis of the Church. It was in this churchly form, without resort to formal public schools, that the Protestant impulse to basic education reached its peak of achievement. Even at this peak, the Protestant dynamic was probably as limited in its achievements in Sweden as it appears to have been in New England, confining its accomplishments to the extent of literacy. The Swedish Church did not intend to modernize attitudes, if anything the contrary, and the evidence from New England suggests that no such psychic changes underlay the revolution in basic literacy led by Protestantism.

The differences between New England and Scottish Calvinism on the one hand and Swedish Lutheranism on the other further illuminate the common features of that Protestantism which led to systematic state action and so to a rapid rise toward universal male literacy. All three of these Protestant societies were quite small, ranging from a half-million to two-millions in size. Yet small size was probably not the essential feature. Most of the societies of the North Atlantic were relatively small, and many were more dense, so state-encouraged education would have had considerable impact in any of them. The crucial point is that these were the three societies which took public action to ensure the education of all men and, in one case, of women. The motive force behind this action was the common Protestant impulse to bring to all men the Word of God, implemented by the intensity of the local Protestantism in terms of its depth, breadth, and uniformity. In New England, Scotland, and Sweden a strong, widespread, and homogeneous Protestantism carried the society into public action to ensure basic education, and thereby carried men into universal literacy, all in the name of the true God.

Much has been made of the Weberian implications of Protestantism, and of the manifold ways this religious impulse is supposed to have led to modernity. The intense Protestantism which led to systematic education, and so to very wide literacy, was not without its overtones of modern statism. In the long run, too, the attitudinal implications of mass literacy may have been quite the opposite of the pious conformity intended by the advocates of the Word. Yet these Weberian echoes should not be allowed to obscure the immediate evidence that, in America as in Europe, in so far as literacy moved rapidly toward universality the prime motive force was the conservation of piety, which by all available measures appears to have succeeded.

In the mind's eye the story continues to the effect that in the modern era powerful social forces everywhere revolutionized the level and meaning of literacy. This is probably true,[151] but the story could be turned on its head, to the effect that the meaning of literacy was never truly revolutionized. In seventeenth-century Sweden a conservative social impulse, Protestantism, achieved a rate of growth in male and female literacy entirely comparable to the rapid rates of increase in nineteenth-century Europe and in the third-world nations today. It has been said that Protestantism was a transitional ideology which mobilized men behind traditional values in order to ease the painful passage into a more modern social era.[152] Would it be too much to infer that among the forces behind the rise in literacy in the modern era there is often a similar and equally effective desire to use literacy to reaffirm traditional values in a time of social transition? This possibility appears to be confirmed by the fact that today literacy does not correlate with modern attitudes in developing nations other than former East Pakistan.[153] Aside from a lack of impact in "modernizing" attitudes, it may be that modern literacy does not even equip men with the skills required to deal with their world. It has been estimated that even in the contemporary United States fully half of persons are functionally illiterate.[154] It may have been a characteristic of society from the very earliest stages of western development right up to the present, that the requirements of functional literacy have continually outrun the skills supplied even by a rising trend of adult literacy or even by universal literacy. In both these respects the world we have lost may have been a foretaste of the world we have gained, but not in the senses usually intended.

Appendix A

The Educational Response
to the American Wilderness

Richard Alterman
with Judy Hanson, Kenneth Lockridge,
and Elaine Wethington

✦✦✦

THE evidence that there was no widespread educational response to any real or perceived threats posed by the American wilderness should be presented more explicitly, so that this uniquely American educational impetus can be removed from consideration.

Again, the hypothesis was best stated by Bernard Bailyn's brilliant exposition of the scholarly issues involved in the history of American education, *Education in the Forming of American Society*.[1] Bailyn suggested that in general "to all of the settlers the wilderness was strange and forbidding, full of unexpected problems and enervating hardships." He proposed that in numerous ways the wilderness tended to shatter the orderly and often extended structure of the European family, thereby threatening to destroy the primary context in which culture had been transmitted from generation to generation. The result was presumably "a

[1] Chapel Hill, 1960; reissued most recently by W. W. Norton and Company, New York, 1972.

[103]

sudden awareness, a heightened consciousness of what the family had meant in education, of how much of the burden of imparting civilization to the young it had borne, and of what its loss might mean." Apprehension apparently led in turn to a series of conscious efforts to glue the family back together and to provide alternative means of education. This newly conscious concern for education, Bailyn concludes, became the cornerstone of an "American" educational ethos.[2]

As the text mentions, there is no evidence that the wilderness shattered the essentially nuclear families which arrived in America. If anything the new environment strengthened family bonds for several generations.[3] Moreover, there is little to distinguish the supposedly wilderness-spurred laws concerning the family and education from similar laws and customs then prevailing in England. Few, if any, of these colonial laws mention the wilderness. Any fear of dissolution one might sense behind such legislation is no more than that vague apprehension for the fate of civilization which the English themselves repeatedly managed to generate without the stimulus of a literal wilderness. There seems to be little basis for a uniquely intense and conscious American concern for the provision of education as a substitute for families sundered by the wilderness.

Bailyn nonetheless maintains that there was a widespread awareness among the settlers "that only by conscious, deliberate effort would the standards of inherited culture be transmitted into the future." He suggests that this reaction was found not only in New England but in the South, where "lacking the reinforcement of effective town and church institutions, the family . . . was even less resistant

[2] *Education*, pp. 22, 26–32, 47–49.
[3] Philip J. Greven, Jr., *Four Generations* (Ithaca, N.Y. 1970), pp. 261–269; unpublished papers on family discipline in colonial Hingham, Mass., by Daniel Scott Smith of the Univ. of Connecticut indicate that loosening of family bonds came as a result of social changes which occurred very late in or after the colonial era.

to pressures and sustained even greater shocks. The response on the part of the settlers, however much lower their intellectual demands may have been than the Puritans', was equally intense. The seventeenth-century records abound with efforts to rescue the children from an incipient savagery." [4] The argument continues to the effect that "the most common [of efforts to rescue children from savagery] were parental bequests in wills providing for the education of the surviving child or children." As examples of these "fascinating, luminous documents" Bailyn mentions the wills of Susan English of York, of Samuel Fenn, and of John Custis.

Is this true? The evidence of several hundred Virginia wills from the seventeenth century is that hardly more than one testator in fifteen left a bequest to education in any form whatsoever. [5] Of testators who mentioned surviving children, only one in ten expressed the faintest concern for education. This feeble consciousness was, however, "equally as intense" as in the northern colonies, where similar samples yield nearly identical figures. Nowhere was there an "abundance" of provisions for education of children. [6]

---

[4] *Education*, p. 28.

[5] Specifically, only 22 of 309 testators left bequests or provisions which even by the most stretched of interpretations could be said to pertain to education. These wills represent an estimated 75–100% of all wills available for Virginia in this period, and a much larger percentage of all wills for the counties sampled—Rappahannock, York, Henrico, and Northampton. The documents are available on microfilm from the Virginia State Library in Richmond.

[6] Roughly one hundred and fifty Connecticut wills from the period 1635–80 (on file at the State Library at Hartford and published in Charles Manwaring, *Early Connecticut Probate Records*, Hartford, 1904–06) and three hundred New York wills from 1660–1700 (printed in *Abstracts of Wills on File at the Surrogate's Office in the City of New York*, 1893), yield gross levels of bequests to education between 5% and 10%. Eighteenth-century samples yield slightly lower figures in all areas. Regional differences in rates are of marginal significance.

TABLE 1: *Concern for Education in American Wills,*
1630–1700

	VIRGINIA	CONNECTICUT	NEW YORK	TOTAL
Mention of education	22	14	15	7%
No mention of education, direct or indirect	287	135	288	93%

None of the rare provisions mentioned the wilderness, and none seems to have involved an effort to rescue children from an incipient savagery. Most bequests were couched in the tones of an ordinary legal arrangement. William Bernsdett of Northampton County, Virginia, provided "that my loving wife Alice shall live in my land and have the charge of the education of my child." Charles Dunn, of York County, Virginia, stipulated that if his wife died the remainder of his estate should go to Robert Calvert, "and my will is that he be brought up well and well educated." The will of Susan English reads in the same manner. A minority of those who provided for education went to some lengths to be sure that their child would be fully educated under assured arrangements, as in the wills of Samuel Fenn and John Custis but, as will be seen, this was a normal parental concern. In general nothing disturbed the even tone of those few Virginians who thought of education, and the same can be said of their counterparts in New England and New York.

These colonists were participating in what was essentially an English tradition. In England, indeed, the wealthy may have shown a slightly more abundant concern for education than these frontier Americans. A sample of wills from the Prerogative Court of Canterbury indicates that over 10% of these relatively prominent Englishmen left provisions for education of descendants or fellow citizens. A more typical sample drawn from the Rochester Archdeaconry Court of Kent yields a level of 6%, which is statistically indistinguishable from that prevailing in wilderness America.[7] Samples from less wealthy regions indicate that the aggregate rate of provisions for education in England could have been as low as 3.5%, which would be only half of the aggregate American rate of approximately 7%, yet in a realistic perspective the conclusion would still have to be that both areas manifested similarly low rates of educational consciousness. The qualitative similarities between American and English bequests are most convincing. The deadpan provisions of dying colonists merely repeated the provisions of their English cousins. "I leave five pounds for the education of my son" was the monument to a man's concern in either environment. In England as in America occasional bequests revaled a burning parental desire to guarantee the best possible education for a child, but in general legalese prevailed.

Bailyn goes on to state that "the extravagance and often impracticality of such efforts in Virginia suggest a veritable frenzy of parental concern lest they and their children succumb to the savage environment."[8] Yet there is nothing to suggest that such bequests to education as did occur in Virginia were either extravagant or impractical. John Waltham of Virginia, for example, provided that "after my son has attained the age of six years he may then be brought up and educated in the sole instructions of good learning, and . . . grounded in the rudiments of scholarship and school learning. My will and desire is that he may

---

[7] A sample of 160 Norfolk, Gloucester, and Kent County wills probated in the Prerogative Court of Canterbury in 1759 and 1760 (representing approximately one-half of all wills from those counties probated in the PCC those two years) shows a 15% rate of parental bequests to education. One hundred wills proved in the Archdeaconry Court of Rochester, Kent, in 1661 yield a 6% level.

[8] *Education*, p. 28.

then be put into school unto some good and godly school-
master, and that especial choice be made of such school-
master within the colony of Virginia." John Waltham's
will makes clear that he was neither an extravagant nor an
impractical man. He knew basic education could be provided in Virginia, and the literacy record of colonial Virginia bears him out. Far from being participants in a
"frenzy," the John Walthams of colonial America were just
doing what their counterparts in England were doing, providing for education. The only remarkable feature is how
few men bothered to imitate their example, on either side
of the Atlantic.

Appendix B

Toward an Ideal Study
of Literacy in Early America

✠

THE shortcomings of this study are generally evident, and they point to tasks which will have to be accomplished by a "second generation" study of literacy.

The Measure

Like the rest of the world outside Sweden, Americans must use signatures and marks as their measure of historical literacy. In general I agree with Roger Schofield * that the level of signatures is always somewhat above the level of writing and somewhat below the level of reading. Gross differences in signature rates should therefore imply real differences in overall literacy. The difficulty is that a large proportion of persons making marks may have been able to read quite fluently, which means that absolute levels of reading could have been much higher than signatures would indicate. Worse, it is possible that in one society a basic education which was confined to reading, or a practice of

---

* All scholars mentioned here are discussed in the footnotes to the text and listed in the Bibliography.

leaving school before writing was taught, could have resulted in a very high proportion of readers among the markers, while in another society essentially no markers could read because all readers had received instruction in writing early in their studies and so could sign their names. The result would be two societies, or social classes, or eras, which had identical levels of signatures yet had substantially different levels of reading. Conversely societies or classes or eras with differing signature rates could have had rather similar reading levels. Similarly deceptive comparisons could arise from a less likely and essentially opposite flaw, namely a substantial and varying proportion of illiterates who learned to sign their names. Either of these flaws would invalidate signatures not only as an absolute but also as a comparative measure of literacy. Indirect research cited in the text and notes of this study indicates that while the proportion of markers who could read may have been quite substantial, neither it nor the small proportion of signers who were illiterate varied much by class or over time within New England. Yet the measure will not be secure until we find in several nations samples of persons for whom we have both signature-mark data and information on actual literacy. Only such a comparison will establish that signatures and marks reflect the same measure of literacy regardless of nation or era.

Helena Hoas is attempting just such an analysis of the meaning of signatures and marks in Sweden. Egil Johansson and I have encouraged her to seek out a sample of persons living in the seventeenth and eighteenth centuries, whose true literacy we can get from catechismal examination records and perhaps from schoolmasters' records, and whose signatures or marks can be found in other local sources. Ironically, we are having a hard time finding a source of reliable signatures and marks. It seems that literate Swedes occasionally made family marks instead of or with their signatures, while imprecise copyists often added a signature when an illiterate person had in reality only made a mark. The remarkable speed with which Sweden achieved literacy is also a handicap, since by the time the records became most ample, after 1700, there are few illiterates left to study. Still, we hope one day soon to be able to report that in Sweden most persons who signed their names could read fluently and perhaps write while most persons who made a mark could neither read nor write, and that this is true for all classes in all periods. Together with the indirect evidence from New England, this should establish the consistency of the measure for comparative purposes. It will also permit estimates of the absolute levels of literacy skills which lie behind a given level of signatures. The Swedish research may even supply a more sensitive measure of literacy by breaking signatures and marks into meaningful subcategories.

The Swedish comparisons of signatures and marks with actual literacy will be continued into the nineteenth century. In theory the same comparison could be made for nineteenth-century America, since signatures and marks are available, and by this time actual literacy was recorded in the Census. The problem is that the takers of the 1840, 1850, and 1860 Censuses seldom bothered to ask the fascinating social questions which were added to these and subsequent surveys. When they did bother, they were often careless. An extremely careful modern interviewer once found that 15% of persons claimed to be able to read when they could not read, so one can imagine what a tremendous degree of optimism must be incorporated in the early Census. The safest generalization is that this would be a comparison of one unassessed measure with another.

Until several reliable comparisons of signatures and marks with actual literacy are made, the measure can be made more secure by combining it with other measures. For example it is fairly certain that any American or Englishman who made a firm signature and whose inventory of estate lists more than two books, at least one of which was not on a religious subject, was literate. Likewise a man who made a crude mark and whose inventory listed no books was probably illiterate. In this way we might derive estimates of fluent literacy and total illiteracy in a given area and use these as the dependent variable in studying local variations, while isolating these most interesting types for further study.

The Sources

A greater problem arises when American scholars turn from the measure to the sources in which it is found. American records do not provide samples as representative as those found in Europe. Nor do they provide as many of the supplementary variables essential to a complete analysis (see Table A, with footnote 2).

Deeds and wills are the main sources available. American law required that all land transactions be recorded in the county courthouses. The resulting deeds should include all landowners, or as much as three-quarters of the adult male population. Each man is found at various stages in his life. The age of the sample is not too much older than the average age for adult males. Deeds often give the residence and the occupation of the landowner, in addition to his signature or mark. So far so good, but unfortunately there are few European documents which are similar enough to permit ready international comparisons. Furthermore the law requiring registration of land transactions was poorly observed in the seventeenth century and was always unevenly enforced in various regions, creating a fluctuating sample which is difficult to assess. Further, even at their best deeds excluded virtually all women and the landless. And deeds lack information not only on wealth but on father's wealth, father's literacy, father's status, exact residence when of school age, and migration. These crucial variables are available only with immense labor in records scattered from the local to the county to the state archives.

Wills are also a mixed bag. From a quarter to a third of men left wills when they died, a proportion which was not substantial but was fairly constant. The occupational distribution is close to that which would be hypothesized for the society. Supplementary information includes above all wealth, and also a list of surviving family members, home village, occupation, charitable behavior, books, and in some cases the signatures or marks of the wife and son. Wills closely parallel equivalent sources in England. On the other hand, the sample *is* far more narrow than that offered by deeds, and it is more biased toward wealth even though it includes a few of the landless. The contrary bias of old age appears to lower the signature rate in wills by a significant amount which is hard to measure. Here too, few women are included. Here too, information on father's literacy, etc., and on mobility is not readily available.

In essence neither American source is as broadly representative as Swedish examination records or English marriage records. Neither seems to offer or to be stored near information on father's condition or on migration, important variables which can be found with the Swedish examination records and with information on literacy in some English depositions and local records. The source which is the most inclusive, deeds, involves samples which are the most uneven and the most difficult to assess or compare, and includes the least additional information. Wills, the source which is the most assessable, and comparable, and which includes the most supplementary information, is by far the least inclusive.

The situation is not as bleak as it seems. Using wills alone, rather less fully than they could be used, I have obtained a profile of literacy in early New England which is close to that which would be predicted for the male population at large and which reveals fascinating changes in the structure of literacy in New England. Such analyses could be extended by blending sources rather as Roger Schofield envisions using the breadth of marriage registers in tandem with the perhaps random samples of some depositions and with the rich information found in depositions, wills, and local records. This will be more difficult and less satisfactory in America where, in addition to the limitations of deeds and wills, legal depositions do not appear to have the special qualities of their equivalents in England. Yet the breadth of deeds could be combined with the deeper analyses permitted by wills and further information attached to the individuals found in these records by a diligent search through local sources. A rationale for combining sources will be discussed below.

The Issues

Within the limitations of the single-source method used here, however, a great deal can be done to resolve the major issues concerning literacy in early America. The pattern of literacy outside New England has not been established by the present research. Too much rests on Virginia. In New York or New Jersey literacy may have been rising well above the 70% mark, erasing all correlation with status and, for all we know, intensifying the "liberated" attitudes of optimistic, individualistic, and enterprising Americans. Our ignorance is fundamental, and on this gross level literacy is rather easy to investigate.

A future investigator should gather large enough samples over a long enough period to be able to speak of local differences in literacy. As Roger Schofield has pointed out, local variations reflect the more subtle forces operating on literacy in this muted social world, forces barely discussed here. Why was one region of eighteenth-century England 80% literate and another only 50%; indeed why was one village 80% literate while its neighbor showed only 50% literacy? In the Virginia counties, why did Westmoreland reach 75% literacy when Norfolk remained around 65% and counties farther west barely surpassed 60%? The regional differences in America are not quite as great as in

England, but once we get on a town-by-town level the variations may approach the order of magnitude found across the Atlantic. Can these variations within American literacy be explained by local differences in the migrant streams and by differences in lesser intensities of the Protestant impulse? Or will we find that even in areas which had no public school system, population concentration entailed an increased access to and perhaps need for education and so raised the level of literacy higher in some localities than in others? Population concentration might explain why newer, more western areas of Pennsylvania and Virginia had lower literacy rates than more concentrated eastern areas, even though those western areas were probably more intensely Protestant. But how could this hypothesis in turn, explain differences between eastern counties all of which had attained a certain minimal level of social concentration? Or must we there turn back to the influence of later migrations and of variations in the Protestant impulse to explain local variations in literacy? One thing only is clear: while the forces of social and economic development do not appear to have been effective in drastically raising literacy anywhere in early America, social forces in some form still had much to do with why one man was literate and another not, and so could have had much to do with why one locality was more literate than another. Social forces, along with variations in the level of a more diffuse Protestantism, may have been very much involved with literacy within limits defined in this study.

In France, it seems that male literacy rose from perhaps 30% around 1690 to nearly 50% by the Revolution. To what do we ascribe this doubling of literacy within a century in a very large population? Hardly to Protestantism (or is that necessarily ruled out?). Hardly to social mobility. Were the forces involved cultural or social? If cultural then Protestantism, operating primarily in smaller societies, was not the sole cultural force capable of achieving very substantial increases in literacy, albeit far short of universality. Professor Lionel Rothkrug of Sir George Williams University is now preparing a comparative analysis of French Catholicism which implies that this religion embodied a non-Protestant cultural imperative with a powerful impact on literacy in France. On the other hand, Professor Charles Tilly has just offered a demographic explanation of the broad secular uptrend of literacy in early modern Europe, an explanation which could account for the quite respectable uptrend of literacy in France in particular (*History of Education Quarterly,* Summer 1973). Whichever explanation prevails, it is evident that there is much more to be said about the forces behind variations and rises in literacy at levels below the near-universal.

So far the talk is entirely of causes, but the effects of literacy will bear as much investigation. I am now bringing larger samples and more unambiguous measures to bear on the non-modernization of social perceptions. The need now is for other such measures of mass attitudes in the past. David Riesman has said that the dead cannot be interviewed, but they can, and results which show change could undermine the thesis of this paper. The economic effects of literacy also bear attention. The hypothesis offered here implies that these were modest at best. Perhaps a mad-dog econometrician would attempt a returns-to-literacy analysis for some eighteenth-century samples. A powerfully increasing economic return to literacy in a context of rising literacy could also pose serious problems for this author's theories both of causes and of effects.

Finally, the level of functional literacy demands should be estimated at various points in time. The technique is essentially that employed by David Harman in his estimate of the level of these demands today. The documents which a man was required to understand should be analyzed to yield an estimate of the number of years of schooling needed to achieve a comprehension of those documents. Changes in this socially necessary level of education, and in the relationship between it and the possible supply of education, will provide an approximation of the functional literacy gap from moment to moment. Here again, this author's hypothesis could be modified and perhaps disproven.

Methods

As the issues get into such esoterica as the sources of literacy, the social and economic returns to literacy, and into the ability of literates or illiterates to function successfully, issues outrun the answers which present methods can provide. The way to a more powerful technique for analyzing literacy in the past has been shown by the historical demographers and tentatively employed by Michael Sanderson and by Egil Johansson. This is simply to reconstitute the entire lives of a sample of families from every available source.

The researcher would use vital records, gravestones, town records, court records, depositions, wills, deeds, contracts, and so forth to construct an ongoing life history of a family. What was the father's occupation, his wealth, his literacy as measured by signatures and by books, his wife's literacy, how many children did they have, how far did they live from a school, what were the school fees, which children became literate, how do their occupation and wealth compare with their father's or with the achievements of illiterate children, and which of their children did these children in turn educate? This focusing of the information from individually fallible sources into the framework of the family, multiplies several times the richness and reliability of the analysis. The price is the loss of families whose histories cannot be adequately reconstituted from the records.

To demonstrate one use of such data, consider the question of whether literacy was acquired in the home or in school. Taking the families in Village A, and treating literacy as the geneticists treat an hereditary defect by coloring in the men ▲ and women ● who have it, we find:

Family 1   Family 2   Family 3

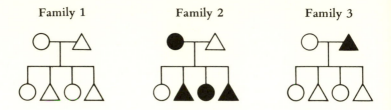

Clearly this is a village in which literacy is acquired only in the home, there only when the mother is literate, and even then the education of daughters is sometimes neglected. In the neighboring and equally tiny village of B, we discover:

Family 1   Family 2   Family 3

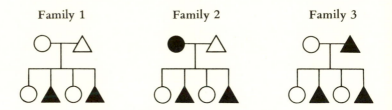

There seems to be a village school which admits only male children, and no home education whatsoever.

The influence of a father's wealth and occupation in the education of his children can likewise be ascertained by this method, as Egil Johansson has shown in his analysis, which points to mere distance from the schoolhouse as a more influential variable. Likewise the relationship between literacy and achieving an occupational status other than the father's can be ascertained, as Michael Sanderson has done, with mixed results.

"The method" involves in reality several stages of analysis. The first is simply to reconstitute enough families to acquire an idea of the range and subtlety of the patterns by which literacy is transmitted. At a more advanced stage the data can be in a sense aggregated (crude results derived) and further explored in order to sort out the crucial variables involved and their relative importance and general relationships. A computer program called Automatic Interaction Detector is designed to do just this, and it is intended for the mixture of hard and soft variables and missing values inevitably found in literacy analyses. In the end, sophisticated causal hypotheses can be tested by the use of another program, Multiple Classification Analysis, also developed at the Institute for Social Research at the University of Michigan.

The reconstitutive method can easily be applied in Sweden, where nearly all the requisite variables are readily associated with most families through the use of only two or three sets of sources. It is through the Swedish sources that we will look most deeply into the nature of literacy in the past. Yet the method can have a great impact in raising the quality of analysis outside Sweden, and it must be applied elsewhere for Swedish results to acquire their full significance.

Bibliography

BAILYN, BERNARD. *Education in the Forming of American Society*. Chapel Hill, North Carolina, 1960.

BANTOCK, G. H. *The Implications of Literacy*. Leicester, 1966.

BLALOCK, H. *Causal Inference in Nonexperimental Research*. New York, 1968.

BOGUE, DONALD J. *Principles of Demography*. New York, 1969.

BOWEN, W. G. "Assessing the Economic Contribution of Education." *Economics of Education*. Ed. M. Blaug. Baltimore, Md.: Penguin, 1968.

BOWMAN, MARY JEAN, and C. ARNOLD ANDERSON. "Concerning the Role of Education in Economic Development." *Old Societies and New States*. Ed. C. Geertz. New York, 1963. Pp. 247–79.

BROWN, RICHARD D. *Revolutionary Politics in Massachusetts: The Boston Committee of Correspondence and the Towns, 1772–1774*. Cambridge, Mass., 1970.

BRUCE, P. A. *Institutional History of Virginia in the Seventeenth Century*. 2 vols. New York, 1910.

BUSHMAN, RICHARD. *Puritan to Yankee*. Cambridge, Mass., 1967.

CIPPOLA, C. *Literacy and Development in the West*. Harmondsworth, 1969.

CLEWS, ELSIE. *Educational Legislation and Administration of the Colonial Governments*. Vol. VI of *Columbia University Contributions in Philosophy, Psychology, and Education*. New York, 1899.

CRAVEN, W. F. *White, Red, and Black*. Charlottesville, Va., 1971.

CREMIN, LAWRENCE A. *American Education*, 1, *The Colonial Experience*. New York, 1970.

DEEN, JAMES W., JR. "Patterns of Testation in Four Tidewater Counties in Colonial Virginia." *American Journal of Legal History*, 16 (1972), 167–69.

Cressy, David. "Education and Literacy in London and East Anglia, 1580–1700." Diss. Cambridge Univ., 1972.

DOLLAR, C., and R. JENSEN. *Historian's Guide to Statistics*. New York, 1971.

"Functional Illiteracy Found High in U.S. in Study at Harvard." *New York Times*, May 20, 1970, p. 1.

FURET, FRANÇOIS. Paper delivered at the Uppsala University Conference on Quantitative Methods in History, June 1973.

GOODY, JACK, ed. *Literacy in Traditional Societies*. Cambridge, England, 1969.

GREENE, EVARTS B., and V. D. HARRINGTON. *American Population before the Federal Census of 1790*. New York, 1932.

GREVEN, PHILIP J., JR. *Four Generations*. Ithaca, New York, 1970.

INKELES, A. "Making Men Modern." *American Journal of Sociology* (Sept. 1969).

JOHANSSON, EGIL. "Kvantitativa Studier av Alfabetiseringen i Sverige." Pedagogiska Rapporter, No. 7 (Umeå, 1969). Pp. 16–26.

—— "Literacy Studies in Sweden." Unpublished paper, 1972.

—— *En studie med kvantitativa metoder av Folkundervisningen: Bygdeå socken, 1845–1873*. Pedagogiska Institutionen. Umeå University, 1972.

KAHAN, ARCADIUS. "Determinants of the Incidence of Literacy in Rural Nineteenth-Century Russia." In C. Anderson and M. Bauman, *Education and Economic Development*. Chicago, 1965.

KILPATRICK, WILLIAM H. *The Dutch Schools of New Netherlands and Colonial New York*. Washington, D. C., 1912.

LANDES, W., and L. SOLOMON. "Compulsory Schooling Legislation." *Journal of Economic History* (1972).

LOCKRIDGE, KENNETH A. "Land, Population, and the Evolution of New England Society, 1630–1790." *Past and Present*, 21 (1966).

—— *A New England Town: The First One Hundred Years.* New York, 1970.

—— "Social Change and the Meaning of the American Revolution." *Journal of Social History* (June 1973).

MORGAN, EDMNUD S. *The National Exerience.* 3rd ed. New York, 1973.

MORISON, SAMUEL ELIOT. *Puritan Pronaos: The Intellectual Life of Colonial New England.* New York, 1936.

SANDERSON, MICHAEL. "Literacy and Social Mobility in the Industrial Revolution in England." *Past and Present,* 56 (1972).

SCHOFIELD, ROGER. "The Measurement of Literacy in Pre-Industrial England." *Literacy in Traditional Societies.* Ed. Jack Goody. Cambridge, England, 1969.

SCHUMAN, H., A. INKELES, and D. SMITH. "Some Social Psychological Effects and Non-Effects of Literacy in a New Nation." *Economic Development and Cultural Change,* 16, No. 1 (1967).

STONE, LAWRENCE. "Literacy and Education in England, 1640–1900." *Past and Present,* 42 (1969).

THOMAS, KEITH. "Women and Civil War Sects." *Past and Present,* 13 (1958).

TULLY, ALAN. "Literacy Levels and Educational Development in Rural Pennsylvania, 1729–1775." *Pennsylvania Magazine of History and Biography* (1973).

UPDEGRAFF, HARLAN. *Origins of the Moving School in Massachusetts.* New York, 1908.

VINOVSKIS, MARIS. "Horace Mann on the Economic Productivity of Education." *New England Quarterly,* 43 (1970), 550–71.

WALZER, MICHAEL. *Revolution of the Saints.* Cambridge, Mass., 1965.

WEBER, S. E. *The Charity School Movement in Colonial Pennsylvania.* Philadelphia, 1905.

WINTER, RALPH D. "Reading in the Guatemalan Environment." Fifteenth Yearbook of the National Reading Conference, 1966. *New Frontiers in College-Adult Reading.*

ÅKERMAN, SUNE, and EGIL JOHANSSON. Report on Literacy and Migration in Nineteenth-Century Sweden. Paper delivered at the Uppsala University Conference on Historical Literacy, May 1972.

Footnotes

1. Bernard Bailyn, *Education in the Forming of American Society* (Chapel Hill, 1960), particularly pp. 1–49; Lawrence A. Cremin, *American Education, I, The Colonial Experience* (New York, 1970), esp. pp. 517–70.

2. See Table A. Wills cover a fairly constant 25–35% of adult males, near the time of death, around age 55. In theory records of land transactions (deeds) kept in each county as required by American law should cover all landowners. Deeds would therefore include the signatures or marks of some 75% of adult males at an average age of around 45. But the proportion of men covered by deeds still excludes the poorest quarter of society; and the rather variable proportion covered actually falls below 10% in many areas in the seventeenth and early eighteenth centuries, when the law was widely ignored. Further, the sample offered by wills can be matched to samples with similar biases drawn from European probate records, whereas deeds have no single European counterpart. Finally, wills and inventories contain more independent variables for analysis than deeds, most particularly wealth. Books listed in inventories of deceased persons' estates offer a different measure of literacy, and inventories are a source which included roughly half of adult males near the time of their deaths. But books seem to reflect literary rather than economic literacy, and there is considerable evidence that books were not always listed in the inventory even when present in the estate. Depositions—testimony given for or in front of a court hearing a case—seem highly selective and usually offer little additional information about the individual.

TABLE A: *Sources for Historical Literacy in America, England, France*

SOURCE	MEASURE OF LITERACY	SAMPLE REPRESENTED	YEARS AVAILABLE	ADDITIONAL VARIABLES	COUNTRY
Wills	Signatures v. Marks*	20–50% of adult males dying 2–5% of adult females dying	In America, circa 1660 on, in quantity. Otherwise universally.	occupation charity family size village of residence	America England France?
Deeds	Signature v. Marks	5–85% of living adult males less than 1% of living adult females	After 1660–1700 in quantity.	occupation village location within village	America
Inventories	Books**	25–60% of adult males dying 3–10% of adult females dying	In America, circa 1660 on, in quantity. Few after 1720 in England. France uncertain.	Same as with wills	America England France?
Depositions	Signatures v. Marks	Uncertain. Potentially more select than wills, potentially wider. Women sometimes included.	In America, circa 1660 on, in quantity. Otherwise universally.	Few in America, but potentially: age occupation sex village of birth village of residence	America England France?

Record Type	Examination/Mark Type	Coverage	Dates	Variables	Additional Variables	Country
Marriage Records	Signatures v. Marks	Nearly all (80%+) young men and women marrying in England after 1754. In France . . . ?	1754 on in England, with more selective and/or isolated records available earlier. Circa 1650 on in France.	occupation age parents' names parents' occupation	sex village of birth village of residence	England France
Catechetical Examination Records	Memorizing examination Reading examination Comprehension examination Writing information in some villages	Unclear, but seems very wide.	Increasingly after 1620.	occupation tax status village of residence parents' names & status	location within village family size migration***	Sweden Finland
Local "Treasure Trove" Records						Seem best in north England

* Reliability and interpretation discussed elsewhere.
** Reliability low, interpretation uncertain.
*** Readily available supplementary records give information on migration, and on others of these additional variables.

Wills, inventories, deeds, depositions, tax records, and accidental finds will have to be used together in an effort to duplicate the information available from European sources. In France, and in England after 1753, marriage registers include both sexes shortly after schooling. The sample appears to be nearly universal and such variables as age, occupation, and parent's residence and occupation are often available. French military records offer a similar source, likewise not widely available in America. Roger Schofield of the Cambridge Group for the Study of Population and Social Structure reports that records unique to certain parishes in northern England may permit easy access not only to literacy but to parents' status. David Cressy of the Pomona-Claremont Colleges is working on literacy as reflected in English depositions, certain classes of which appear to yield a virtually random sample of men and in addition offer information on migration, age, and occupation. The best records of all are in Sweden, where the reading and comprehension skills of each family member were recorded periodically, on forms which also included such information as location and taxes paid. Egil Johansson of the Department of Education at the University of Umeå is analyzing these records.

3. The assumptions behind this interpretation of signatures are that as the general level of reading skills rises, the level of "acceptable" or "fluent" reading rises, that an "acceptable" or "fluent" reader could at least sign his name, and that some of these (alone) could also write. A related assumption is that persons who could not read could not sign their names. My own research confirms these assumptions; the exceptions are usually trivial and often tend to cancel one another. Lawrence Stone and Roger Schofield more or less share these assumptions about the measure (both have made investigations) though Stone's interpretation is somewhat more flexible. See Lawrence stone, "Literacy and Education in England, 1640–1900," *Past and Present*, 42 (1969). For Schofield, see "The Measurement of Literacy in Pre-Industrial England," in Jack Goody, ed., *Literacy in Traditional Societies* (Cambridge, England, 1969).

One example of the validity of these assumptions: if men who could not read somehow learned to sign their names, the level of signatures could rise with no real increase in literacy; yet if this happened, the proportion of "doubtful" or "unskilled" signatures on original documents should also increase; and in fact this small proportion does not increase with time despite a rising trend in signatures. An inverse example is the common claim that distinguished and literate men often made "marks" which were really personal signets, thereby causing the investigator to overestimate illiteracy. Careful study reveals that such men were less than .5% of all cases.

The ultimate confirmation that signatures (and indeed signatures on wills) measure literacy, will be found in the statistical correlations of signatures with sex, wealth, occupation, and location of residence, discussed in the body of this essay. Signatures correlate with all these variables exactly as a measure of literacy would be predicted to correlate—down to the subtlest gradations between occupations. The same appears to be true of signatures found in all sources whatsoever.

In a recent paper delivered at the Uppsala University Conference on Quantitative Methods in History in June of 1973, François Furet reports strong evidence that, at least in France, signatures correlate to a high degree with the ability to read and write, as would be expected under the interpretation used in this manuscript. Thus evidence from England, America, *and* France points to this interpretation.

Women may be the exception to these definitions. They continued to be educated in reading alone long after the educational reforms of the seventeenth century had added writing to the primary curriculum for males. So in theory women exposed to education could read fluently without being able to sign their names, since they had had absolutely no exposure to the written alphabet. And in theory there could be a substantial increase in women's reading skills with no change in their signature level. But there is a contrary bias where women are concerned. Since they acquire delicate motor skills in the household, women are able to "fake" a smooth signature when totally illiterate, a trick men rarely acquire. David Harman, formerly with Israel's literacy program, has encountered this phenomenon. It is confirmed by the fact that only one-third of a sample of women signing their names to wills owned books. The result is that women may show a high and increasing level of signatures when their actual literacy is low and unchanging. Research now underway in Sweden (see text, below, and Appendix B, on future analyses) may resolve this and other contradictory possibilities in the interpretation of signatures. Meantime, women's signatures will be interpreted exactly as men's.

Papers by François Furet and by Roger Schofield, delivered at the Conference on Quantitative Methods in History at Uppsala, and subsequent correspondence with both scholars, give no reason to alter the decision to take women's signatures at face value. Schofield and this author do agree that it is possible that at some point a high proportion of women making marks could read fluently. There is, however, some reason to believe that this high frequency of reading among women is a phenomenon which evolved only at the very end of the period here under consideration. (Even if it evolved earlier, and specifically in Protestant areas, this phenomenon would not entirely alter the passive association between Protestantism and female literacy deduced in this manuscript. It would become true that Protestantism did perhaps significantly increase the level of reading skills among women, even to a level not far beneath that of the male population.

Yet it would remain true that in most Protestant areas women were regarded as mere passive receptors of the written Word of God. The capacity to respond was, from all the evidence of the signatures, generally reserved for men.)

4. The main sample of 3126 wills is representative of colonial New England wills and includes roughly one-ninth of them. It is made up of essentially all wills probated in Fairfield and Hartford Counties, Connecticut, in Hampshire, Suffolk, Middlesex, and Essex Counties, Massachusetts, and in New Hampshire and Maine, during the years 1650–70 (ca. 700 wills), 1705–15 (ca. 1000 wills), and 1758–62 (ca. 1400 wills). These areas were broadly representative of New England and contained over one-third of its population. The periods sampled include nearly one-third of the years of the colonial era. Each period encompassed a mixture of economic conditions.

Official court copies were used. These copies were chronologically intact from week to week and showed less than 2% error on all variables combined. The use of copies made it impossible to code varieties of signatures and marks, but subsamples of original wills revealed serious problems with such classifications, problems whose resolution will have to await research now underway in Sweden, in which the author and other scholars are comparing signatures and marks to actual literacy. Coding copies was twice as fast as coding original wills. Variables coded include charitable behavior, literacy, sex, occupation, county of residence, urban-rural residence, inventoried wealth where readily available, and in some cases family size.

Men constitute 85% of the sample. Men who left wills represent a constant 25–35% of all adult males dying in the counties and periods selected. They were not radically unlike the hypothetical male population in occupation, as 60% were farmers, 20% artisans, and the remaining 20% were equally divided among laborers, shopkeepers-merchants, professionals, and gentry. They were more often urban residents, 20% as against 10% in the population, which created a slight bias toward literacy. But their major biases are age and wealth. Men leaving wills averaged around 60 years old as against an average of perhaps 45 years for the adult male population. Partly because of their age, these men were also twice as wealthy as men who left no wills but whose estates were inventoried at death.

Less than 15% of the sample were women, and they represented less than 5% of all adult females dying in the counties and periods selected.

Numerous subsamples have also been taken. The largest is drawn from Suffolk and Middlesex Counties, Massachusetts, from 1787 to 1795. Evaluation of all samples has been painstaking. There is no room to detail the enquiries pursued into the realms of sampling theory, probate law, and demographic and economic history.

Footnotes

5. There was a tendency for the wealthy to write their wills earlier than other testators, so these "feebleness" rates derived from ministers and gentry could be too low for the whole sample. A lesser toll of feebleness among upper-class testators would also exaggerate their literacy relative to farmers, etc. Yet these possibilities seem of minor import for several reasons. The ministers, at least, were not extremely wealthy and in fact did not write their wills significantly earlier than an equal-size group of farmers worth £100–400. In this respect the 2% for marks presumably caused by feebleness among ministers should be fairly typical of all classes. Moreover, quite sharp differences in the time the will was written would result only in rather small differences between classes in the toll of feebleness. If only 15% of the gentry made their wills after the point at which terminal palsy was likely to afflict them, and 40% of the farmers did so, how much difference could it make? Assuming that one man in three who made his will within this "feebleness eligible zone" actually fell prey to feebleness before making his will, then the *maximum* number of marks-due-to-feebleness which the gentry would make would be roughly 5% (one-third of 15%) as against some 13% among farmers (one-third of 40%). The actual toll of literates-made-markers-by-feebleness would be lower in each case, however, since some of the 5% of gentry and 13% of farmers struck by feebleness would already be illiterate. Assuming 1 in 20 real illiteracy among gentlemen and 1 in 5 among farmers, the proportions of literates-made-markers-by-feebleness would fall to 4.75% for gentry (5% minus the 1 in 20 already illiterate) and roughly 10.5% for farmers (13% minus the 1 in 5 already illiterate). The upshot would be an added difference in the signature rates of the two classes of only some 6% (10.5 minus 4.75), and the necessity of raising the 5% estimated toll of feebleness derived from the gentry to no more than 9% to more accurately estimate the toll for the whole sample. These are modest effects and there is no evidence of class differentials in the time of writing wills as great as those used in this calculation, at such crucial breaking points as one month or three months. The research into Swedish sources mentioned in n. 2 is designed to explore the effects of age on literacy as well as to get the basic meaning of signatures and marks, so it may further resolve this issue.

6. A similar trend has been found in Virginia, where the proportion of testators whose wills were probated less than one month after being written fell from over 20% in 1660–79 to below 15% in 1700–19 and by extrapolation below 10% in 1760. One problem is that such a trend may not reflect an increasing interval from the writing of the will to death, and so may have had no effect in reducing the toll of feebleness: the dispersal of the population could have created a situation in which an increasing proportion of wills were simply probated

ever longer after the death of the testator because of an increase in the time required to bring the will to the central registry of probate. This possibility aside, a shift of as much as 15% of testators out of a "feebleness-eligible-zone" (assuming that one-third of the persons in this zone actually delay their wills until too palsied to sign their names, and depending on the literacy rate in the sample) could mean as much as an absolute 5% decrease in literates-making-marks-out-of-feebleness. For Virginia data see James W. Deen, Jr., "Patterns of Testation in Four Tidewater Counties in Colonial Virginia," *American Journal of Legal History*, 16 (1972), 167–69.

7. Ann McMillan (University of Michigan, 1972) did this research. All the men who "forgot" were Boston artisans, so if forgetting was class-specific its effect was to understate the relative literacy of this class. There were no cases of forgetting among rural farmers, even though they "should" have been more prone to forget since they lived in a relatively uncommercialized environment. Forgetting may have been more frequent among women and may have remained common among women after it disappeared among men, but the sample is small and the adjustments indicated would not affect the conclusions of this study. The research underway in Swedish records should clarify this phenomenon, but meantime it will be assumed that there were no class or sex differences in "forgetting." (Incidentally, David Cressy ["Education and Literacy in London and East Anglia, 1580–1700," Ph.D., 1972, Cambridge University] also encounters evidence of "forgetfulness," indicating that it is a real bias in data which includes many older persons, a bias requiring significant adjustments. Hence, while not huge, the phenomenon is one to be reckoned with.)

8. This is based on the actual trend in New England, projecting the literacy of men dying around age 60 in 1695, 1745, and 1795, back to 1660, 1710, and 1760 when these men were age 25. In every case these "25-year-olds" alive in 1660, 1710, and 1760 show a signature level an absolute 5–10% above that of the cohort dying in these same years.

9. Research into the published probate records of seventeenth-century Essex County, Massachusetts, is largely consistent with this estimate. Russell Garland (University of Michigan, 1972) finds that some 10% of men made marks on wills which were fairly well articulated or were actually initials and owned more than two books. (This includes a substantial allowance for men whose books were not recorded in their inventories.) At this time another 10% of men made an elaborate mark or initial and owned one or two books *or* made a simple mark yet owned more than two books. Hence a total of 20% of men (at this time, 50% of markers) made marks on their wills yet

showed convincing indications of some ability in literacy. The figure for women is of the same magnitude. While it is doubtful that feebleness and forgetfulness can account for more than half of these persons, the surplus merely points up the likelihood that *in any source* a certain proportion of markers are persons who could indeed read though they never learned to sign their names and most likely were not fluent readers.

10. The evidence of dwindling influence is mentioned in the preceding text. It is confirmed by the fact that as of 1760 ordinary farmers (£100 to £400 wealth) in some localities had a level of marks below 15% in their wills, making it manifestly impossible that the biases of age could have led 15% of them to make marks!

The same general figures can be used for women. Their levels of feebleness and forgetfulness were probably higher but they were not subject to opportunity lag since their literacy trend was not sharply up. The decline was probably less distinct among women.

11. Goodman and Kruskal's Gamma, a measure of association between ordinal variables, ranged from .450 to .800 depending on the categorization of wealth employed, when wealth was cross-tabulated with the measure of literacy used here. The men in the sample averaged twice as much inventoried wealth as intestates whose estates were inventoried. The value of Gamma for wealth versus signatures declined from around .700 in period I (1660) to well below .500 in period III (1760). For Gamma see C. Dollar and R. Jensen, *Historian's Guide to Statistics* (New York, 1971), p. 82.

12. The interpretation of signatures offered earlier was a deliberate middle way between attempts by opposing interpreters respectively to maximize and to minimize the quantity of literacy represented by a given level of signatures—albeit a middle way confirmed by such evidence as is available. In the case of adjusting for the biases of wills, the middle way of balancing age against wealth and occupation is simply a result of the best independent estimates of these biases which could be made. For those who would bend this result upward or downward, there are certain facts to consider. The researches of David Cressy confirm work by this author and his students that there is a real but not overwhelming downward bias associated with an aged sample. One student's estimate places this bias at circa 5% (see n. 7 and related text). Both in Virginia and elsewhere wills yield signature rates around 10% below the rates in deeds, and age appears to be the major net bias of wills vs. deeds. Hence it seems impossible to avoid the conclusion that because of age the signature rate in wills is biased downward *something* on the order of 5 or 10 or at most 20 per cent. On the other side, the estimate of a 5–20% upward bias due to wealth

and occupation tends to result no matter what parameters or methods are used to derive an assessment of this bias. There is some evidence that the effects of the former, and firm evidence that the effects of the latter bias are declining with time. The tug of interpreters from either side notwithstanding, it is hard to escape the conclusion that these biases largely balance and that signatures in wills correspond roughly to the level of signatures in the population at large. The plausible exceptions to this assumption do not affect the conclusions of the paper.

13. The thing to do is to track men who left wills and men who died intestate into another source, such as deeds, and find their relative signature rates. But the samples would have to be fairly large to permit controlling for the effects of wealth, occupation, etc.

14. See n. 10.

15. This assumes that of twenty-five adult women ten would live to become widows.

16. Nn. 3, 4, 7, 10, and text immediately preceding, sum up the problems of evaluating the meanings of women's signatures on wills.

17. See the chapter on "New England Literacy in Comparative Perspective."

18. Whenever the signature rate of one subsample is compared with that of another, it may be assumed that the difference (or similarity) in literacy rates commented upon is not likely to be accidental and that it meets the usual statistical tests of "significance" (here set at .95) where these are relevant. Exceptions will be denoted by such words as "tends" or "seems" and specifics supplied in a footnote.

Also, many minor inconsistencies in the data—for example on one occasion male signatures in period 1 will be set at 61% and on another 60%—are caused either by rounding off in the text as opposed to the graphs or by the fact that for certain variables information is available only for a subsample whose literacy may not exactly match that of the total sample. To take the most extreme case, wealth is known for only a 40% subsample, whose literacy happens to be lower than that of the sample as a whole. Thus, when discussing the interactions of wealth with literacy, the literacy figures cited will tend to be a little low.

19. Unassessed sampling error and congenital illiterates could account for as many as 5% marks in any sample, so a rate of 95% signatures would amount to universal male literacy.

20. Samuel Eliot Morison, *Puritan Pronaos: The Intellectual Life*

of Colonial New England (New York, 1936), pp. 82–85. Morison cites studies of signatures made by William Kilpatrick and Clifford K. Shipton, and a study of signatures in Virginia by P. A. Bruce. See William H. Kilpatrick, *The Dutch Schools of New Netherlands and Colonial New York* (Washington, D.C., 1912), and P. A. Bruce, *Institutional History of Virginia in the Seventeenth Century*, 2 vols. (New York, 1910).

21. Morison's *Pronaos* discusses these laws.

22. As Morison is well aware; *Pronaos*, p. 84.

23. Shipton (petitions) replied to an enquiry from the author, confirming that he did not entirely control for the repetition of names. Kilpatrick (deeds) does not discuss the issue, but there is reason to believe that he too failed to prevent this bias: P. A. Bruce, the only scholar cited by Morison who states that he counted each name just once, derives a signature level from Virginia deeds, etc., which is only 10% above the data from Virginia wills used later in this study; this is precisely what would be expected when repetition of names is controlled for and the only difference in the sources is the age of persons leaving wills, which creates a downward bias of this magnitude; the implication is that Kilpatrick's 95% figure from Massachusetts deeds, which runs 35% above the figure for Massachusetts wills, is indeed inflated by the recurrence of literates.

Failure to control for repetition resulted in a signature rate 25% above the actual rate, in one study of probate records. The bias was roughly equivalent in a large sample of deeds. It may be less in the case of petitions, but there is evidence that the wealth bias of petitioners is actually greater than that among will-leavers. Women's signature rate is not greatly affected by failure to control for repetition, since women rarely appear repeatedly.

24. The alternative is to explain the 35% discrepancy between wills (60%) and petitions, deeds, etc., entirely in terms of the biases of age which lower the signature rate in wills. Yet repeated investigations find no grounds for setting the effect of such bias above 15%, leaving at least a 20% unexplained discrepancy between wills and petitions, deeds, etc. Repetition of literates in the counts of petitions, etc., supplies a sampling error known to have been made and of the proper magnitude to explain this discrepancy. Furthermore, the eventual rise in signatures on wills from 60% to 90% dramatizes the inflation of the 95% estimate for this early period, for this rise would have been impossible if wills had a 35% negative bias because of old age. The only possible conclusion is that the old 95% figure was grossly inflated for one reason or another and that estimates based on wills are more accurate.

25. Morison, *Pronaos*, p. 85.

26. Actually, signatures as interpreted in this article can lead either to a minimum or to a maximum estimate of literacy. On the one hand it is possible to assume that many persons making marks could read, perhaps fluently, on the ground that signature is a very difficult skill almost equivalent to the ability to write. This also implies that most signers could in fact write and would make it unlikely that any signatures were mere copies produced by illiterates. The result is a logically consistent interpretation which tends at every point to maximize the levels of reading and writing. In the case of earliest New England, this would mean that virtually 60% of males would be able to write as well as read, well over 60% would be considered fluent readers, with the number of total illiterates running from 10% to 20% depending on conditions such as those mentioned in the text. On the other hand, if signing is considered relatively easy, then surely anyone who could read at all could also sign, regardless of the formalities of the educational system. This would mean that all markers were essentially illiterate. In such a case, signatures might even include a few illiterates who had copied their signatures. In the case of earliest New England, this would mean that well under 60% of men could write, rather less than 60% could read fluently, perhaps a little less than 60% could read at all, while more than 40% were totally illiterate. Until the research into Swedish sources settles these ambiguities, compromises such as those reached in the text will have to suffice.

27. Morison was aware of the weaknesses of the data he used, and though his book did somewhat idealize its subjects, he would have been the first to admit that the question of literacy was open. For the attitudes associated with illiteracy, see Jack Goody, ed., *Literacy in Traditional Societies* (Cambridge, England, 1968). The aside on the lessened contrast between settlers and environment is a reference to the "environmentalist" school of educational history, best represented by Bernard Bailyn's *Education in the Forming of American Society,* which holds that a uniquely conscious American educational ethos arose from the shock created by a wilderness which threatened to undermine all the achievements of education. This issue will be taken up in subsequent sections of the text.

28. The only effect of controlling out these shifts (which exist both within the raw sample and within the subsample used to estimate the effect of the generally high level of wealth and occupational status on the signature level of the sample, hence are very much an integral part of the data structure) is to lower the literacy level in period II by several percentage points. This in turn accentuates the relative rapidity of the rise in male literacy after, as compared with

before, period II, thereby strengthening a major point to which attention is already directed. These shifts over time toward higher wealth, etc., do not appreciably affect the level of literacy in period III, however, since by this time wealth, etc., had very little impact on the level of signatures.

29. See text preceding.

30. The farmers were worth from £100 to £300 and made brief wills within three months of probate. These conclusions are strengthened by the causal analysis developed in the next section, which shows that the causal forces behind the rise in literacy in the sample were apparently forces which would have acted on all men.

31. For example, see Morison, *Pronaos*, p. 68.

32. See n. 28. The "elbow" in the trend is confirmed by spot samples drawn between 1680 and 1700 and again between 1720 and 1750. Its significances will be discussed below, in the section on causation.

33. Small samples drawn by some investigators yield male signature rates approaching 100% as early as 1760. See, for example, Lawrence A. Cremin, *American Education, I, The Colonial Experience,* 526. These exaggerate the speed with which New England achieved universal male literacy. Cremin neglects to allow for the disproportionate wealth of his sample, an adjustment which would bring male literacy in Dedham back toward 92%. And Dedham was a populous town with a long tradition of concern for its schools, quite unlike more feckless areas of New England where signature rates were lower. The New England male signature rate was probably closer to 85% than to the 97% in Cremin's Dedham sample.

34. Two of the five, New Hampshire and Maine, involve samples too small to justify more than saying that the trend seems to be faster after 1710 than before. The data from Hartford, Hampshire, and Essex Counties are more reliable.

35. Again, the changes and differences in literacy rates and correlations with literacy discussed here meet the required tests of statistical significance (set at .95) where these are relevant. Major exceptions will be noted.

36. To be exact, more than 90% of the increase in literacy took place among rural farmers, artisans, and laborers. The remainder is accounted for by minor improvements in the already high literacy of merchants, shopkeepers, and urban artisans, in a trend which is of dubious significance.

37. This powerful trend among farmers may, however, have been more continuous than among males in general. Farmers too had their fastest rate of improvement immediately after 1710, with their adjusted rate nearly double the previous rate, but they showed more improvement than other groups before that date and the initial rise among farmers remains significant even when the effects of their increasing wealth are removed. In the overall sample this early improvement among farmers was somewhat dampened by an initial decline in the signature rate of the gentry and further slowed by a slower initial rise among other nonfarm groups. Still, most of the large minority of the sample not identified as to occupation, were almost certainly farmers and were certainly rural, and this minority definitely shows post-1710 rate of improvement more than twice that of the 1660–1710 period, so the *relative* consistency of trend among those identified as farmers is somewhat deceptive.

38. Maine, New Hampshire, and Essex and Hampshire Counties showed a rate of improvement half again as fast as Suffolk, Middlesex, and Hartford Counties. Yet these former low-literacy areas continued to have a lower per capita wealth than the other counties, likewise averaged fewer books per male testator, and had demonstrably lower population densities—not to mention that they had probably been founded by migrants with lower literacy rates than was the case in other localities. The equalization of their literacy with that elsewhere may be measured by the weakening correlation of region with literacy: in period I this correlation was on the order of .500 (Gamma) and by period III it had fallen to .150.

39. The difference between farmers (44%, n=200) and "upper crust" (94%, n=75) is statistically reliable and the differences between farmers and artisans, and artisans and laborers, very nearly meet the standard of statistical significance imposed here.

40. Because the later sample is larger, the differences in literacy rates between occupations are of nearly the same order of reliability as in 1660; and it is probably not accidental that the literacy hierarchy still has the same rank order as the occupational-status hierarchy. Nonetheless, the strength of the relationship (i.e., the probability that a lower status would involve illiteracy) had fallen from circa .650 (Gamma) in period I to circa .350 in period III and was evidently still falling.

41. n=100, 200.

42. The initial (1660) difference between the over £500 line on Graph 5 and an aggregate of the two under £200 lines is reliable, though any given difference between adjoining groups may not be,

because of the small samples. Nonetheless (here as with status) the consistency with which the rank-order of these social variables is duplicated by the rank-order of literacy in all periods indicates that in fact differences in literacy rates by status or by wealth group were real. As for the change with time, the graph can be better expressed in terms of correlation coefficients: period I literacy versus wealth = .600 (Gamma); period III = .300, using a slightly different categorization of wealth from that on the graph. Here too the correlation was apparently still decreasing.

43. Alex Inkeles et al., Harvard Project on Social and Cultural Aspects of Development. See in particular H. Schuman, A. Inkeles, and D. Smith, "Some Social Psychological Effects and Non-Effects of Literacy in a New Nation," *Economic Development and Cultural Change*, 16, No. 1 (1967); also see A. Inkeles, "Making Men Modern," *American Journal of Sociology* (Sept. 1969), for the broader framework of the entire project.

44. Schuman, Inkeles, and Smith, "Some Social and Psychological Effects and Non-Effects of Literacy . . ." define literacy as "reading slowly but with general comprehension" or a higher level of skill. This is close to my own interpretation of signature-literacy.

45. Schuman, Inkeles, and Smith, p. 7.

46. Inkeles, "Making Men Modern."

47. Bernard Bailyn, *Education in the Forming of American Society*, pp. 48–49.

48. Lawrence Cremin, *American Education*, I, *The Colonial Experience*, pp. 546–50. The text here is an attempt to clarify an argument which, while more explicit than Bailyn's, is far from precise.

49. Again, see Inkeles, "Making Men Modern," and the works cited therein.

50. Richard D. Brown, *Revolutionary Politics in Massachusetts: The Boston Committee of Correspondence and the Towns, 1772–1774* (Cambridge, Mass., 1970).

51. Or so I argue in "Social Change and the Meaning of the American Revolution," *Journal of Social History* (June 1973).

52. Admittedly, Mann's appeals were varied and may bear only an oblique relation to his true aims. For a discussion of these issues, see Maris Vinovskis, "Horace Mann on the Economic Productivity of Education," *New England Quarterly*, 43 (1970), 550–71.

53. This evidence, and subsequent intimations that neither literacy nor time was "modernizing" men's attitudes in eighteenth-century Virginia either, may seem to contradict not only the current historiography of American education but indeed the author's own previous works: *A New England Town: The First One Hundred Years* (New York, 1970) suggests that a moderate degree of spatial and social differentiation in eighteenth-century Massachusetts may have been preparing the way for a liberation of human attitudes from the traditional, local, organic matrix; "Social Change and the Meaning of the American Revolution," envisions such differentiation, augmented by the Revolution, leading to a small national constituency for an ideology of pluralism akin to that finally offered by James Madison in *The Federalist*, No. 10.

Yet both *A New England Town* and "Social Change . . ." are clear that the social forces involved were moderate and that any attitudinal changes were (respectively) latent or confined to a small minority. These modest arguments are perfectly consistent with the continuance, and indeed even the enhancement, of traditional attitudes in most areas of the lives of most Americans. Specifically, they are consistent with the evidence that charitable attitudes remained traditional. The case made in these earlier publications should in no way be misconstrued into the massive and conscious modernization of human attitudes which others have seen in eighteenth-century America.

As for the nineteenth century, a case could be made for massive changes in human attitudes, changes perhaps unique to America. Yet one could also make a case for the continued existence of a traditional localism which was indeed enhanced in reaction to the changes of this century until there emerged a monumental counterpoint of old and new which is truly characteristic of America.

Complete results on the correlations between charitable attitudes, time, and literacy will be presented in a separate article as soon as a sample of wills from 1815 to 1820 is analyzed, along with the data from Virginia and from England which is mentioned below. A subsequent article will discuss the anatomy of charitable giving in the three areas and seek to explain its decline.

54. A similar argument applies to the potential economic effects of the rise in male literacy. Mary Jean Bowman and C. Arnold Anderson ("Concerning the Role of Education in Economic Development," in C. Geertz, ed., *Old Societies and New States*, New York, 1963, pp. 247–79) have reviewed the data on developing nations and concluded that literacy and the complex of social changes associated with rising literacy seem to correlate with a definite increase in per capita income. Indeed, a literacy level of 40% seems to be prerequi-

site to an average per capita income exceeding $300. Above this level up to the 70% literacy level, literacy correlates only weakly with economic development. The correlation is restored at literacy levels above 70% and something like 90% literacy appears to be a prerequisite of per capita incomes surpassing $500. There is logic in these findings. If literacy and the skills and attitudes associated with it do not spread beyond a minority, even a commercial economy will be handicapped. Beyond this point the spread of literacy is not as important to further economic development as is the emergence of other and often more advanced skills. Yet whatever this development, the ultimate modernized economy cannot thrive if a significant portion of the population remains illiterate, hence the second threshold. In this perspective, however, colonial New England constitutes an exceptional case. Here was a society which from the beginning had all the literacy its simple commercial economy could require. Its founders were well across the first threshold of literacy when they arrived and their gains were never lost despite the dispersal into the wilderness. New England crossed the threshold of mass literacy sometime before the American Revolution. It had achieved the basic educational prerequisite of full economic modernization. With the Protestant ethic coupled to mass literacy the population of New England represented a fantastic potential for economic development. Yet that development did not immediately take place, and for sound reasons it would be unwise to expect immediate economic effects from colonial New England's evolution into mass literacy. The modern data suggest substantial economic effects from the growth of literacy through the 70% to 90% range only because these data describe modern economies which already possess most of the requisites of economic development and in which residual illiteracy blocks maximum growth. Such was not the case in colonial New England. The other requisites of economic development were missing. A substantial minority of illiterates had probably not been a serious block to growth in the simple commercial economy of the day, so the mere elimination of this minority could not be expected to produce an economic surge. These suppositions are confirmed by the fact that a large subsample shows the usual increase in literacy entirely without a rise in per capita wealth. Economic development like attitudinal change was chiefly a prospect whose way mass literacy prepared but which could not arrive until other conditions were ripe.

55. Students of American history will be aware that social protests arising from what was in effect functional illiteracy were still strong in the nineteenth century, as the free-coinage-of-silver movement attests. There is good reason to believe that, while the quality of literacy has since risen, the functional demands of society have

risen further, leaving the nation today with a wide "literacy gap." See the *New York Times*, May 20, 1970, p. 1, "Functional Illiteracy Found High in U.S. in Study at Harvard." If mass literacy produces anomie and cultural insecurity as well as activism, as is suggested by G. H. Bancock, *The Implications of Literacy* (Leicester, 1966), these queasy attitudes could have mingled with the frustrations of functional illiteracy in a ferment of discouragement quite unlike the flow of active optimism usually anticipated from mass literacy.

56. Some 75 women dying before 1670 averaged 31% signatures as against 44% for 350 women dying 1705-92.

57. Roughly 100 women dying 1705-15 averaged 41% signatures, which was improved to only 46% by the 250 women dying 1758-92, and some of this marginally significant rise may be caused by distortions in the sampling (see note on Graph 7). Nonetheless, the possibility of a slow rise should not be ruled out, especially since other contingent patterns are taken seriously in these pages.

58. The data cited in Morison, *Pronaos*, p. 83, more or less substantiate these levels found in wills; his examples are perhaps 10% higher, but this is no more than would be expected because of the relative downward age-bias of wills.

59. The precise levels and rates of change in rural male and female literacy are not at issue in this description, but rather the implications of gross differences by sex in level and rate of change which appear to be statistically reliable and reliably more distinct in the countryside.

60. Boston = 75 women 1650–1715 average 40% signatures; 75 women 1758–92 average almost 65% signatures. This increase nearly meets the standard of significance imposed in this study. The remaining gap between men and women in Boston is less reliable but is probably not an accident of the sample.

61. See note 3, last paragraph, for a possible but only partial qualification to this view.

62. Again, the implication that education in general or literacy in specific accelerated the modernization of attitudes in certain senses can be found in Bernard Bailyn, *Education in the Forming of American Society*, pp. 47–48, and in Lawrence Cremin, *American Education: I, The Colonial Experience*, final chapters; Bailyn and Cremin also assume or logically must assume that there was a general increase in literacy to quite high levels, as a reflection of the power of the same educational ethos which was changing attitudes and as a necessary

way of access to those new attitudes. For the specific case of New England, see text and n. 63 immediately following.

63. This is the hypothesis of Bernard Bailyn, *Education in the Forming of American Society*. Bailyn is explicit that the New England school laws involved this "more than Puritan" concern for education, that the schools were perhaps most effective in the seventeenth century, and that literacy is a good measure of their achievement (pp. 27, 83, 84). While he is skeptical of literacy measured by signatures, he does not repudiate the results cited in Morison's *Pronaos*, which indicate that the schools may have widened the extremely high literacy of the migrants and that male literacy was essentially universal toward the end of the seventeenth century. Bailyn further speaks of the parallel evolution of a dynamic educational ethos elsewhere in America and of the typical optimism, individualism, and enterprise it produced everywhere in colonial America (p. 48). This related thesis virtually requires rising and quite widespread literacy elsewhere in America, if it is not seriously to be questioned. As will be seen, neither in New England nor in the rest of America are the requirements of these hypotheses met. This is true not only of the full hypothesis as offered by Bailyn but also of the more specialized version of it offered by Cremin, *American Education* (pp. 545 et passim), in which the stress is almost solely on social mobility as a causal force behind high literacy and "liberated" attitudes. Insofar as Cremin would apply this argument to explain the growth of literacy in colonial New England, it does not seem to work either.

64. Morison, *Pronaos*, p. 59.

65. Because it is a question solely of searching for possible causal relationships within the sample, the statistical significance of the relationships involved in this discussion is not crucial. As it happens nearly all the patterns discussed are significant to .90 and most to .95.

66. It might help to translate these samples' dates into the "real time" in which people were educated in literacy. The sample of 1660 was largely educated between 1595 and 1625, that of 1710 between 1640 and 1670, that of 1760 between 1690 and 1720, and that of 1790 between 1720 and 1750. The single years in which the largest proportion of each sample was educated in literacy should fall around 1615, 1660, 1710, and 1740, respectively. (Assuming that the adult male population was on the average twenty years younger than the sample and so educated in literacy twenty years later, the modal dates at which the contemporaneous male populations received their educations in literacy would be 1635, 1680, 1730, and 1760.) Whether in the sample or the population, the generation educated in England showed a literacy rate of 60%. A subsequent generation born and raised in seven-

teenth-century America at least equaled this rate and may have surpassed its progenitors. The greatest improvement came among that generation educated early in the eighteenth century. The increase continued among those educated on the eve of the Revolution, but it slowed as literacy became total.

The modal dates for the sample were derived as follows. A man dying in 1660 at age 55 (the assumed modal age at death in the period) and educated in literacy at age 10, received that education in 1615. A man dying in 1710 at age 60, and educated in literacy at age 10, was educated in 1660. A man dying in 1760 at age 60 and educated in literacy at age 10, was educated in 1710. Etc., etc., etc. The assumptions are that the modal age at death was 55, 60, 60, and 60 in each period, and that men were educated in literacy at age 10. The distribution of adult ages-at-death around the modal age at death is such that over 75% of each sample is likely to have been educated in literacy within the thirty year spans given in the paragraph above; see Donald J. Bogue, *Principles of Demography* (New York, 1969), p. 558.

67. Lawrence Stone, "Literacy and Education in England, 1640–1900."

68. Roger Schofield, paper delivered at the Uppsala University Conference on Historical Literacy, May 1972.

69. In theory it could, for local populations in early seventeenth-century England did attain male literacies on the order of 60% (see Stone, pp. 100, 110), so the entire Puritan minority in England could have attained such a level. Migration would therefore have involved transporting a representative segment of the Puritan community to New England.

70. Sune Åkerman and Egil Johansson, Report on Literacy and Migration in Nineteenth-Century Sweden, delivered at the Uppsala University Conference on Historical Literacy, May 1972.

71. The power of such a process may be overestimated here. The raw male literacy rate of 60% has been used for convenience, but the best indications are that this might have been closer to 55% once exact adjustments for age and wealth were made, and residual bias could bring it as low as 50%. The use of raw data therefore tends to exaggerate slightly the degree to which selectivity and migration produced a literacy rate above the English average.

72. The rank-order coefficient was .825, a measure of the agreement of the order of literacy rates by county in 1710 with the order

prevailing in 1660. (With Hartford excluded the correlation rises above .900.)

73. It is unlikely that continuing migration from England explains the 1710 rank-order as sampling indicates that less than 10% of that sample was born or educated in England. Large internal migrations within New England would probably have scrambled rather than reinforced the rank-order of literacy by counties. Even if one or both of these phenomena do explain the 1710 rank-order of local literacies, the fact would remain that neither school laws nor the wilderness determined that rank-order.

74. The original literacy of the settlers and the degree to which they transmitted their literacy were of course related to their wealth and occupation levels. These, plus the degree to which they transmitted their literacy, in turn affected the wealth and occupational distributions among their descendants. Hence the rank-order of counties in literacy is very close to their rank-orders in wealth and in high literacy occupations, both in 1660 and 1710.

75. See Philip J. Greven, Jr., *Four Generations* (Ithaca, New York, 1970) for one example of recent evidence that the wilderness did not initially nuclearize an extended family inherited from Europe, or even further nuclearize nuclear families, as Bailyn, *Education,* has suggested.

76. Richard Alterman, a graduate student in the School of Education at the University of Michigan, reached these conclusions after analyzing more than 5000 wills in early America and England. His results run contrary to Bailyn's suggestions in *Education,* p. 28. Alterman's work will be published in 1974. For further details see Appendix A.

77. See n. 63. Also, many of these data are reported in the text, Graph 2, and notes of the previous section. Even if the rise in backwoods areas is explained in terms of subsequent, more literate migration, the fact remains that the wilderness did not dissolve literacy in the backwoods.

78. Bailyn, *Education,* p. 27.

79. The preface to the law is quoted in Morison, *Pronaos,* pp. 67–68, and his judgment is delivered on p. 59.

80. This generation showed a male literacy of 69% as against 61% for the previous sample. The fact that a portion (not over 33%) of the 1710 sample was educated in literacy prior to the adop-

tion of the school laws in 1647 and 1650 is of little consequence, as it is well known that immediately prior to these laws the bulk of the population lived in towns which had already established public schools on their own authority. Hence laws wrought no dramatic change in the real conditions of schooling. At most, the question should be rephrased to say "why were the *schools* initially so ineffective," so as to embrace the minority of the sample living when these schools existed but not the laws which made them official. (Incidentally, use of the law to confirm an existing educational practice—in this case public schools—was repeated in the nineteenth century, when the law requiring attendance at school merely confirmed widened attendance. See "Compulsory Schooling Legislation," by W. Landes and L. Solomon, *Journal of Economic History*, 1972.)

As mentioned in n. 75, the proportion of English-born and educated men in the 1710 sample seems to have been under 10%. Even if it were several times as high the literacy rate of English-born persons would have to differ quite radically from that of native New Englanders to move the indigenous rate much below or above the 69% assumed here. Thus, if 20% of the sample were English-educated and were 75% literate, native literacy would fall only to 67%. If 20% were English-educated and were 60% literate (by then the ordinary rate in those parts of England which yielded most migrants to New England) native literacy would rise only to 71%. In any case a 1710 subsample known to have been born in New England showed the same circa 69% rate as the total sample, so the point is moot.

81. The small period 1 sample for New Hampshire makes it unwise to claim that its progress was as rapid as Graph 2 would indicate, but it is fairly safe to say that there was a rise at least equal to the New England average.

82. See the results reported in the next chapter.

83. This and the following results derive largely from a multiple (linear) regression analysis in which literacy is the dependent variable. The chief purpose of the analysis is to determine the correlation of one or several independent variables with literacy, while controlling for the impact of other independent variables. Various intervalizing techniques and dummy variables have been employed to get around the fact that non-interval variables have been used in a form of analysis which assumes interval level data. While statistical significance is not really at issue, nearly all the relationships discussed meet the standard of significance imposed here (.95). In all cases intricate use of simple correlation matrices can be and has been employed to confirm the results of multiple-regression analysis. The net bias of the analysis as applied to this data is to understate the strength of the

various relationships discussed, both because the variables are not optimally categorized and because the relationships involved are not necessarily linear.

In the case of sex and literacy a simple correlation coefficient on the order of .300 is not significantly reduced by controlling for the impact of wealth, county of residence, and urban-rural residence. The resulting partial correlation coefficient is slightly lower in period II (1710) than before or after, as noted in the text.

84. See the text of the preceding section, where it is noted that each of these variables correlates significantly with literacy when the other is held constant. Similarly the correlation of each with literacy is reduced but remains significant when the other, and the remaining independent variables, are controlled in the regression.

85. There is a significant but small (.100) partial correlation co-efficient between area of residence and literacy, i.e., once the effects of wealth and occupation are controlled out. By contrast, wealth and occupation each show partial correlation coefficients as high as .250, and these are reduced by the fact that the actual relationships involved are not strictly linear (see graphs 9 and 10). But, as is observed below, these coefficients do not represent exclusively causal influences on literacy, as in the case with sex.

86. W. G. Bowen, "Assessing the Economic Contribution of Education," in M. Blaug, ed., *Economics of Education*, 1 (Baltimore, Md.: Penguin, 1968), 70, 79–80.

87. The models are Literacy $\longrightarrow$ Occupation $\longrightarrow$ Wealth, versus Wealth (as surrogate for father's wealth) $\longrightarrow$ Literacy $\longrightarrow$ Occupation. If the first model is valid, asymmetrical measures of correlation should indicate that wealth depends more on occupation than occupation on wealth, and probably that wealth depends more on literacy than literacy on wealth. Somer's Dxy and Dyx indicate exactly this, even though the biases built into this measure predispose toward opposite results. Further, an elementary "path analysis" shows that the average of the correlations between literacy and occupation and between occupation and wealth is higher than the correlation between literacy and wealth, as would be expected from the first model. Whereas, in the case of the second model, the average of the correlations between wealth and literacy and literacy and occupation is lower than the correlation between wealth and occupation, which would not be predicted if the model is valid. See H. Blalock, *Causal Inference in Nonexperimental Research* (New York, 1968), p. 73. The path in the first model could be reversed, to read Wealth $\longrightarrow$ Occupation $\longrightarrow$ Literacy, except that Somer's Dxy and Dyx indicate this is a less likely direction of dependency.

88. Actual regressions using sex, wealth, and location in a sub-sample which is 50% female, and using wealth, occupation, and location in a male sample, yield variations explained (R^2) on the order of 20% for 1660 and circa 15% for 1710. Since sex and occupation are mutually exclusive, they cannot be used in the same regression, so no R^2 can be derived which reflects the impact of both of these important variables. Moreover, as observed earlier, the categorization of the variables is often clumsy or unavoidably dichotomized and the non-linear relationships which seem to be involved are not fully described by the linear assumptions built into the multiple regression program employed. Given these considerations an R^2 of 25% (slightly higher for 1660, slightly lower for 1710), seems closer to the maximum permitted by the variables included in this analysis. (Later regressions have in fact yielded this R^2 for regressions using sex *or* occupation with recategorized wealth and location variables, so the maximum R^2 may be closer to 30% when the contributions of sex and occupation are considered together.)

89. As I recall, the famous Coleman Report on variations in achievement among black and white school children managed an R^2 on the order of 50%.

90. See, for example, Morison, *Pronaos*, p. 82.

91. See the Comparative chapter, following.

92. Within this conclusion several models of the educational process could fit the data. A perfectly plausible model would say that at all times 33% of both male and female children were educated at home by literate mothers, while an accelerating proportion of male children over and above this 33% were educated in public schools which at all times took only males. Alternately, absolutely all education could have taken place in the schools initially, with schooling being of limited availability but relatively non-discriminatory, while later schooling's availability widened for men alone. All such models are difficult to test but each has somewhat different implications for the initial locus of education and for the timing of public discrimination, so further work should be done.

The major point made for purposes of this study is that it is probable that most of the increase in male literacy early in the eighteenth century took place in the public schools. This could be because these schools came to be more widely available to men (alone) *or* because men had increased reason to use these schools, or both. The hypothesis does not even estimate the relative weight of these two avenues—availability or choice—which made the schools effective. Interestingly, to the extent it was choice, it is possible that the public schools were never as discriminatory as they seemed. It just happened that women had a low and constant reason to attend while men had a high and in the eighteenth century a rising reason. So not only the mix of private and public education, and the timing of discrimination, but even the degree to which public education ever discriminated against women, is left wholly or partly open.

By 1719–21, even New Hampshire had some sort of school law, in time to affect the literacy rate of the 1760 sample. As New Hampshire's earlier (and statistically imprecise) rise and the lateness of these laws indicate, however, literacy could rise to some degree and/or to some point without school laws. Other forces were involved, as will be pointed out. On the New Hampshire laws, see Elsie Clews, *Educational Legislation and Administration of the Colonial Governments*, Vol. VI of the *Columbia University Contributions in Philosophy, Psychology, and Education* (New York, 1899).

A final observation: in many senses a system of home education would make the major thrust of this account even more powerful, as home education is the most traditional system imaginable. The data simply do not bear out a home education model.

93. To the degree that the following analysis is valid, it also tends retrospectively to validate the assumption that the schools were the locus of the rise in literacy, for the forces in the analysis work largely through the schools.

94. The farm/non-farm percentages are as follows: 1660, 60/40; 1710, 45/55; 1760, 55/45. The percentage of the sample worth more than £500 (the level above which literacy always tended to rise steeply to universality, indicating that this level of wealth might require literacy) was: 1660, 22%; 1710, 27%; 1760, 40%. Were they not statistically independent of the rise in literacy, such shifts would be of the right magnitude to have caused and/or resulted from that rise. The method by which independence is established was discussed in the previous section describing the rise in literacy. Essentially it involves "normalizing" the distributions of wealth and occupation on the distributions prevailing in period I, and finding that this does not reduce the rise in literacy more than several points. See the following textual discussion of Hartford and Middlesex Counties, for more concrete evidence that increases in wealth and in non-farm occupations were not causes (or results) of increased literacy.

95. "Irrespective" of wealth both because controlling out increases in wealth leaves the rise in literacy intact and because in some areas farmers showed no increase in wealth yet manifested the usual rise in literacy. See the discussion of Hartford and Middlesex Counties in the text below.

96. Again, the normalization involved discarding less than 10% of the period II sample and still less of the sample for period III.

97. In periods I and II the partial correlations for wealth and occupation with literacy were as high as .265, while by period III they were consistently below .100 and, in the case of occupation, of borderline significance.

98. The fact of dying in 1760 instead of in 1660, represented by a dummy variable called T_3, has a partial correlation coefficient of .300 with literacy once the other variables in the data are controlled. By contrast, the fact of dying in 1710 instead of 1660, labeled T_2, carries a marginally significant partial correlation with literacy on the order of .100. When T_3 involves dying in 1760 versus 1710 (instead of versus 1660), its value is little reduced.

99. The rank-order correlation of literacy by county in 1760 with literacy by county in 1660 (or 1710) was on the order of .500, as compared with a correlation of .825 for 1710 with 1660.

100. The counties are ranked in literacy such that a superiority of more than an absolute 2%, with county samples each larger than 200, is required to rank one county above another. Otherwise a tie is scored. The same standard is applied in the ranking of social concentration. The rankings are:

	FAIR-FIELD	HART-FORD	ESSEX	HAMP-SHIRE	SUF-FOLK	MIDDLE-SEX	MAINE	NEW HAMP-SHIRE
Concentration	1	2.5	2.5	8	4	6	5	7
Literacy	2	2	2	4.5	4.5	6	7.5	7.5

The correlation is on the order of .700 depending upon the adjustment for ties. Interestingly, the major violations of the rank-order of literacy predicted from the rank-order of concentration are in Hampshire County and in Maine, where literacy samples are smallest (94 and 31 respectively) and most likely to throw off literacy estimates.

101. For what it is worth, militia lists in Evarts B. Greene and V. D. Harrington, *American Population before the Federal Census of 1790* (New York, 1932) indicate that in 1690 both counties had around 85% of their population in towns at or above 350 persons (70 militia) but Essex had over 60% of its population in towns over 500 (100 militia) as against 48% for Middlesex. Since American population doubled every twenty-five years, this difference could have grown considerably by 1710. No further data are available, however, until 1765—the data used in the correlations discussed in the text.

102. Again for what it is worth, the rank-order of counties in percent-living-in towns-over-500 as measured in 1690 militia lists cor-

relates with the rank-order of counties in literacy in the 1760 sample at around .600. The argument is that this correlation intensified by 1710, when the 1760 sample was educated. Here too, no further data are available until the 1765 Massachusetts census.

103. Calculations based on the data in Greene and Harrington, *American Population*. These calculations will be discussed in more detail below, n. 107.

104. This is probably the explanation of New Hampshire's second-fastest rise in literacy, for this area began perhaps twenty points below the average so forces making for literacy naturally had more impact.

105. This is based on analysis of the 1790 sample for Boston.

106. What gives some pause here is the fact that local variations in the wealth of the 1710 sample correlate closely with local variations in the literacy of the 1760 sample. This may simply be because local variations in social concentration produced both higher wealth and higher literacy without the wealth causing the literacy. Certainly local variations in literacy remain after local variations in wealth are controlled out, and the remaining variation still correlates with social concentration. Yet it would be rash to conclude that higher wealth played no causal role in local variations in literacy. And if it did so, how can this be squared with the evidence that increased wealth played no causal role in the general rise in literacy?

107. One way to calculate this is to project backwards the census-based 1760–90 growth curves for all New England towns. Another is to use Greene and Harrington, *American Population*, to estimate from militia rolls, etc., the proportion of the population living in towns below or around 250 persons at various points in time up to the mid-eighteenth century whereafter census data permits a precise estimate. Still another is to combine the foundation dates for towns with Greene and Harrington's militia, etc., lists to estimate the proportion of New England's population living in towns more than fifty years old, on the ground that nearly any town this old would contain more than 250 persons. All methods give similar results, whether the size is 250, 350, or 500. The process of concentration continued in the later eighteenth century, though of course above the threshold most relevant to literacy. Between the censuses of the 1750s and '60s and those of the 1770s and '80s, the proportion of the population living in towns over 1000 continued to rise in Hartford, Fairfield, New Hampshire, Essex, and Suffolk Counties. See Greene and Harrington, *American Population*.

108. Harlan Updegraff, *Origins of the Moving School in Massachusetts* (New York, 1908), pp. 150 ff.

109. Updegraff, *Moving School.*

110. Egil Johansson, *En studie med kvantitativa metoder av Folkundervisningen i Bygdeå socken, 1845–1873* (Pedagogiska Institutionen, Umeå University, 1972).

111. See Richard Bushman, *Puritan to Yankee* (Cambridge, Mass., 1967); but especially Kenneth A. Lockridge, "Land, Population, and the Evolution of New England Society, 1630–1790," *Past and Present,* 21 (1966); Lockridge, "Social Change and the Meaning of the American Revolution."

112. Arcadius Kahan, "Determinants of the Incidence of Literacy in Rural Nineteenth-Century Russia," in C. Anderson and M. Bauman, *Education and Economic Development* (Chicago, 1965), presents quite plausible evidence for a model in which such a rise in rural literacy is spurred by a pressure (and/or wish) to participate in commercial transactions, but leaves unclear the degree to which the spur depends upon economic progress.

113. Research by Judy Hanson and Richard Alterman.

114. Research by Judy Hanson and the author.

115. See n. 92.

116. Among men, the variation in literacy explained by the variables measured falls from around 20% to below 5%, both because of the reduced variation in the dependent variable and because more of the remaining variation is random. This random variation removed, however, there would remain a powerful correlation between wealth at low levels and literacy, as Graph 11 demonstrates.

117. Why was the minority of illiterate males left behind? Was it because forces which were bringing universal male literacy to New England discriminated against the poor? Probably not. The rate of improvement in literacy of an under-£100 sample was virtually identical with that of men with £200–£500 estate (Graph 5). Discrimination if any was slight. Obviously discrimination alone cannot be blamed for the fact that the poor were the last group to show substantial illiteracy.

Rather, the mechanics of the process are to blame. The poor started less literate. All groups improved at roughly the same rate. The result was simply that shortly before 1760 all higher groups had improved right into total literacy while the poor, who had begun lower, still had some improving to do. Discrimination, if any occurred, merely accented this quirk of the process which brought mass literacy to New England.

All nations moving into total literacy doubtless experience a similar moment, when only the poor are left with substantial illiteracy rates and illiteracy is momentarily equated with poverty. The social significance of that moment remains to be discovered.

How long did that moment last? Projected ahead, the literacy rate of New Englanders under £100 would surpass 90% by 1810. This implies that poor persons educated around 1760 and politically influential circa 1780–1810 would have been essentially literate as a group. So the moment when poor men alone still showed substantial illiteracy rates, a moment which began around 1730, was probably over by 1780. Again, it is no more clear whether the passing of that moment made for social consensus or for conflict, than it is whether the moment itself had or did not have disruptive effects. Arguments can be offered either way, and should be.

There are slight indications that the moment lasted longer than 1780. Fragmentary data for Middlesex and Suffolk Counties show no further improvement in the literacy rates of poor males. They seem to have remained isolated at two-thirds to three-quarters literacy. If this was the case, and if the proportion of men under £100 estate in Boston continued to grow as it had between 1710 and 1760, a partially illiterate lower class may have become a growing feature of the urban scene.

118. The partial correlation coefficient for sex and literacy rises above .400 in a period III sample with equal numbers of both sexes, and all other variables have negligible coefficients. This continuing discrimination against women runs somewhat contrary to the thesis of Keith Thomas, "Women and Civil War Sects," *Past and Present*, 13 (1958).

119. Even the role played by social concentration has been minimized, most notably by Lawrence Stone. In conversation with the author, Stone has pointed out that certain ways of adjusting for the biases of age, wealth, and occupation can yield an uptrend in male signatures which is almost as rapid before 1710 as after. He suggests figures on the order of 50% (1660), 60% (1710), and 75% (1760). These are within the range of possibility. Such figures would imply that the spread of literacy began before social concentration could have had its fullest impact. In this view the Puritan school system itself receives more of the credit for this rise in literacy, particularly for the rise in the first generations, and the retarding effect of social dispersal is dismissed. It remains possible but less necessary that increasing social concentration aided in the later stages of the rise in literacy as it encountered resistance near the threshold of universality.

120. Michael Sanderson, "Literacy and Social Mobility in the In-

dustrial Revolution in England," *Past and Present,* No. 56 (1972), pp. 75-104, specifically 103. Sanderson *is* willing to entertain the possibility that in the eighteenth as opposed to the early nineteenth century, literacy and social mobility were interrelated. He provides evidence for this conclusion. Yet in his own summary (103) he does not stress this, and the evidence from New England is that in the eighteenth century mobility was not necessary, either as a cause or as effect, to a rise in literacy.

121. Again, see Bailyn, *Education,* and Cremin, *American Education.* A lesser but related optimism concerning the level of literacy elsewhere in America has been expressed by Edmund S. Morgan in the popular textbook *The National Experience,* 3rd ed. (New York, 1973), p. 65: "the rate of literacy (compared to that of England and the rest of Europe) was high throughout the colonies. . . ."

122. Alan Tully, "Literacy Levels and Educational Development in Rural Pennsylvania, 1729-1775," *Pennsylvania Magazine of History and Biography* (1973). Tully's sample includes virtually all wills probated in Chester and Lancaster Counties between 1729 and 1775.

123. See n. 20. Bruce, also controlling for the repetition of names, found a 5-10% higher signature rate in the late seventeenth-century Virginia deeds-and-depositions (mostly deeds) than the author has found in Virginia wills, which is to be expected since deeds in particular have approximately the same upward wealth and occupation biases as wills while lacking the downward age bias of wills, and it is this bias which creates the lower rate in wills. Once wills are adjusted up to this level, the sources would agree, although both would still have to be adjusted downwards to compensate for the unusually high wealth, etc., of the samples they represent. This will be discussed in the text and notes below.

The wills in the author's Virginia sample include essentially all surviving wills probated 1638-70 in Virginia at large, all wills probated 1670-80 in Middlesex County, probated 1705-15 in Middlesex and Westmoreland Counties, probated 1720-28 in Middlesex, Westmoreland, and Richmond Counties, 1747-49 in Middlesex, Westmoreland, Richmond, and Albemarle, 1758-62 in Middlesex, Westmoreland, Richmond, Albemarle, and Amherst, 1771-73 the same with additional data from Loudon, Orange, and Amelia Counties 1763-90, and probated 1788-97 in Middlesex, Westmoreland, Richmond, Albemarle, Amherst, Loudon, Orange, and Amelia Counties.

124. This assumes that the biases of the sample represented by wills are the same in Pennsylvania and in Virginia as in New England. Calculations indicate that the proportion of men leaving wills was roughly similar in all three areas, averaging 15-30% of males dying,

hence the selectivities of wills are likely to be equivalent. The small net upward bias has been ignored previously in this paper so as to leave the raw data intact, but is introduced here, chiefly as a reminder of its existence and possible role.

125. William H. Kilpatrick, *The Dutch Schools of New Netherlands and Colonial New York*, pp. 196–98.

126. S. E. Weber, *The Charity School Movement in Colonial Pennsylvania* (Philadelphia, 1905), p. 14.

127. Of seventy Virginia men leaving wills before 1650, thirty-two or 46% signed their names. The Oath of 1652 was signed by a broader sample of men who should therefore have shown a lower signature rate. Their higher rate is probably attributable to the fact that, as compared with a group of will leavers dying in the 1630s and 1640s, the signers of the Oath included a high proportion of men who had arrived in the 1640s and early 1650s. Presumably these later migrants were substantially more literate. For the Oath, see the *Virginia Magazine of History*, 39 (1941), 33-36. The continuing flood of migrants into Virginia in the 1640s, '50s, and '60s is described in W. F. Craven, *White, Red, and Black* (Charlottesville, Va., 1971). Even as corrected by Edmund S. Morgan in the *Virginia Magazine* (1972), the population increase figures for Virginia leave little doubt that the bulk of men who signed the 1652 Oath were migrants to Virginia, and not sons of earlier migrants.

128. Again, as is plain from Craven's book, cited in the previous note, the vast bulk of Virginia's population growth 1640–60 is ascribable to migration rather than to natural increase. Hence not only the signers of the 1652 Oath but also men leaving wills 1670–80 were weighted toward migrants, and toward migrants who had arrived more recently than men leaving wills before 1650.

129. Within the reduced sphere left for forces indigenous to the other colonies, one thing is certain, which is that fear of the wilderness played essentially no role. As migrants continued to pour in, those earliest migrants who had families evinced no fear whatsoever that the raw environment required a special effort to ensure the education of their children. Thousands of wills from New York, Pennsylvania, and Virginia reveal no statements of apprehension. The level and language of provisions for education are the same as in New England and in England. This is based on the researches of Richard Alterman, described in Appendix A.

130. Again, most of this data, and conclusions similar to those drawn here, can be found in Allan Tully, "Literacy Levels and Edu-

cational Development in Rural Pennsylvania, 1729–1775." The sample from the 1790s has been drawn by the author's research assistant.

131. Westmoreland, Albemarle, Amelia, and Middlesex Counties.

132. In general this paper assumes (and previously has largely ignored) a net downward adjustment of 5% for the biases of wealth and occupation once the biases of age are removed. But two or three minor refinements of the adjustment process (such as the fact that age is less of a downward bias outside New England where the trend of literacy is level, and the fact that late in the eighteenth century the positive correlation of wealth, etc., with literacy is weak in New England but is still strong elsewhere) indicate that by the end of the eighteenth century the raw data for Virginia and Pennsylvania should be lowered by as much as 10% as against closer to 5% in New England.

133. Stone, "Literacy and Education in England, 1640–1900."

134. One could add that an educational ethos which was a force for social change should have been able to raise literacy toward universality even in the face of a massively illiterate in-migration, and that the widespread impact of such an ethos depended upon its ability to do just this.

135. Tully, "Literacy . . ." reviews educational facilities in eighteenth-century Pennsylvania and concludes that despite their number and increase, they were evidently inadequate to cope. He appears to have reached conclusions similar to this author's.

136. The samples in Graph 14 are too small for the absolute levels of literacy for each wealth group to be certain, but the relative levels of literacy are remarkably stable over time despite quite small samples, as is shown by the fact that in all four periods with one exception the rank-order of the four wealth groups correlates perfectly with their respective rank-order of literacy.

137. Cremin, *American Education.*

138. Cremin and Tully seem to think that data from wills in the 1770s tests the existence of an educational efflorescence in the 1750s and 1760s. This cannot be, as men dying in the 1770s were educated in the 1720s. Hence the data from post-1800 Loudon, Orange, Norfolk, Charles City, and Westmoreland Counties in Virginia represent the first test of the hypothesis. The data confirm Tully's conclusions. Theodore Babcock, a student at the University of Michigan, has very kindly supplied the Virginia data as an adjunct to other research he and Leslie Babcock are conducting.

139. In a paper delivered at the Uppsala University Conference on Historical Literacy, May 1972. The data are primarily from marriage registers, which include a far more representative sample than that found in wills, so should require relatively little adjustment.

140. Stone, "Literacy . . .," p. 121. The 1720 point on his graph would correspond to an adult male generation educated late in the previous century, as he too used marriage registers.

141. This involves a cohort of men age 10 in 1800, marrying around age 25 in 1815, at which time their signatures are entered on marriage records.

142. The text earlier discusses the assessment of these biases in New England wills. Nn. 124 and 132 explain the sample represented by wills elsewhere and detail the relative adjustments recommended for eighteenth-century wills in New England and elsewhere.

143. As measured by Schofield in 1754 ff. marriage registers. Their American counterparts are picked up in 1790 ff. wills.

144. Cremin reaches toward this conclusion, *American Education*, I, p. 549. Here he discovers that his earlier examples of 70–100% male literacy rates throughout colonial America have to be adjusted downward into the 60–70% range to allow for their extreme biases, and that English literacy was in this range. He then undertakes a discussion of the quality of literacy in England and America, at first seeming to assert that literacy was "liberating" in both nations, but increasingly writing as if it were somehow more liberating in America (pp. 547–551). As will be seen, there is little evidence that literacy evolved a new attitudinal structure in either nation.

How long did America and England continue these virtually identical literacy rates? In England there was no detectable improvement until the cohort born after 1790, educated around 1800, marrying circa 1815, and dying around 1850. Rapid improvement toward universal male literacy waited for the generations born after the mid-nineteenth century. Near-universal literacy was a creature of the last decades of the nineteenth century. For America the answer is not clear. The rise to an 80% (unadjusted) signature level in Loudon and Orange Counties among the generation born just prior to 1750 and dying after 1800 might suggest the potential for a more immediate improvement in America. Perhaps the arrival of the nineteenth century brought a golden age of near-universal literacy throughout America, nearly a century before England reached this level. Yet too much can be read into local variations. If Loudon and Orange reached 80% signatures around 1800, a raw figure which would adjust to a figure below 75%, the fact is that the north of England had very probably attained the same rate of signatures at the same time (Scho-field, Uppsala paper). Locally high rates are not necessarily harbingers of a rising trend. Census data indicate that America, too, was well into the nineteenth century before reaching the threshold of universal male literacy.

145. This pattern can be seen in the Virginia data, in data from 1000 contemporaneous English wills coded by the author, and in data gathered by Stone in "Literacy." It also appears in earlier data ana-lyzed by David Cressy, "Education and Literacy in London and East Anglia, 1580–1700."

146. The English wills are a 50–100% sample of all wills with in-ventories available in the various ecclesiastical courts for the Counties of Gloucester and Norfolk in the 1660s, 1700–20, and 1755–65. These do not (yet) include wills proved in the Prerogative Court of Can-terbury. These wills, largely of the most wealthy persons, might show a more sophisticated pattern of attitudes, yet it is already clear from early samples of PCC wills that these persons will not much alter many of the conclusions presented here.

147. The common features of this attitudinal world are so strik-ing that it would be a diversion to stress the variations within it. This is more true since the English sample is not complete, the phe-nomena at hand are subtle, and other measures in the data have not yet been analyzed. A guess would place Virginia deepest in tradition, with the strongest emphases on persons linked to the family (40% of gifts), on persons in general (85% of gifts), on the village (99%), and a strong emphasis on mere alleviation (ca. 95%). England shows the least focus on persons (ca. 40%), but among those fewer personal gifts there is a stronger relative emphasis than anywhere else on persons connected with the family, and with time the emphasis on persons of all sorts is increasing. The reciprocal of the English de-emphasis of persons is a focus on causes which is the highest of any of these samples (60%), but again this is decreasing with time. Within gifts to causes a higher proportion than in Virginia go outside the village (5%). At the same time mere alleviation absorbs a larger pro-portion of gifts than elsewhere (99%). The picture is quite mixed, and it must be remembered that the testators not yet included in this sample (Prerogative Court of Canterbury and later eighteenth cen-tury) are more likely to show more abstract, wider, and constructive consciousness. New England surpasses all areas in its de-emphasis of persons connected with the family (only 15% of gifts). While some of this is simply displaced onto other persons, there is greater stress on abstract causes than in Virginia. This stress is increasing with time, although it has not yet advanced beyond including half of all thoughts and so possibly has not reached the maximum achieved in

England. The proportion of gifts within this category which go out-side the village is the same as in England (5%). Above all, significant rehabilitative giving is found only in New England (>10%). New England's mild interim superiority in attitudes might be ascribed to the same Puritanism which led it to excell in male literacy. If this was the case it emphasizes that within this early Atlantic world those areas which lacked Puritanism were slightly more traditional. See Tables 6 to 12. As in previous tables and citations of data, most of the relationships or non-relationships taken from these tables would pass tests of significance at the .95 level, where these are appropriate. Exceptions are generally noted by the use of qualifying adjectives. The issues raised by this data are the subject of the author's current research. Improved samples should be in, and more sophisticated analyses of these and other attitudinal variables implicit in the data completed, in 1973, whereafter a report will be published.

148. Stone, "Literacy," provides the information on Scotland.

149. Based on papers given by Egil Johansson of Umeå University, with specific reference to "Kvantitativa Studier av Alfabetiseringen i Sverige," *Pedagogiska Rapporter*, No. 7 (Umeå, 1969), pp. 16–26. Also Egil Johansson, "Literacy Studies in Sweden: Some Examples," unpublished paper, 1972.

150. For modern rates, see C. Cippola, *Literacy and Development in the West* (Harmondsworth, 1969).

151. See again Inkeles, "Making Men Modern," and C. Cippola, *Literacy and Development in the West*.

152. Michael Walzer, *Revolution of the Saints* (Cambridge, Mass., 1965).

153. Personal report from Howard Schuman, former member of the Inkeles Project. In Guatemala, at least, it is not just any conservative "transitional" ideology which may be keeping the meaning of literacy traditional, but Protestantism itself, which is there a primary source of intensive literacy. See Ralph D. Winter, "Reading in the Guatemalan Environment," *New Frontiers in College-Adult Reading* (Fifteenth Yearbook of the National Reading Conference, 1966), pp. 1–12.

154. See n. 55. None of the above is contradicted by John Uno, *History of the Baptists in Virginia* (Richmond, unpublished), a copy of which is available in the Virginia Baptist Historical Society, located in the library of the University of Richmond.

All references to pages 1–101 are to the text. References to pages 103–157 are to the appendices, bibliography, and footnotes.

Index

moving, 67, 149
population concentration and, 44–45, 48, 51, 62, 67
reasons for establishing, 4
social concentration and, 62–71
taxpayers' cost, 66
Puritan concern for education, 6, 43, 44–45, 46, 48, 49–51, 58, 64, 69, 72, 73, 74, 86, 97–101, 105, 141, 142, 143, 151, 157
Puritan Pronaos: The Intellectual Life of Colonial New England (Morison), 132–133, 134, 135, 140, 141, 143, 146
Puritan school laws, *see* New England school laws
Puritan to Yankee (Bushman), 150

Quality, need for in literacy, 36–38, 87, 101, 116–117, 139–140

Rappahannock County, 105
"Reading in the Guatemalan Environment" (Winter), 157
Regional differences, end of in literacy, 21–22
Rehabilitative gifts, 33, 35, 36, 86, 87, 96
Religion, as sole source of rise in literacy, 6
Repetition of names, 133
Report on Literacy and Migration in Nineteenth-Century Sweden (Åkerman and Johansson), 142
Residence, 52, 126, 128, 145
association with literacy, 56, 126–127
given in deeds and wills, 112–113
Revolution of the Saints (Walzer), 157
Revolutionary Politics in Massachusetts: The Boston Committee of Correspondence and the Towns, 1772–1774 (Brown), 137
Richmond County, 78, 152
Riesman, David, 116
Rochester Archdeaconry Court of Kent (England), 107
Rothkrug, Professor Lionel, 116
Rural literacy, increase in, 21–22

Sanderson, Michael, 69–71, 117, 118, 151–152
Schofield, Roger, 87, 109, 113–114, 126, 127, 142, 155, 156

School fees, 117
Schools, *see* Public schools
Schuman, H., 137, 157
Scotland, 5, 46, 99, 100
Scots-Irish migrants, 78–83
Sermons, 15
Sex, literacy and, 52, 56–57, 128, 145, 146, 151
correlation of signatures to, 126–127
see also Women's literacy
Shipton, Clifford K., 133
Shopkeepers, 128, 135
Signatures, *see* Wills, signatures on
Sir George Williams University, 116
Slaves, 93, 94
Smith, Daniel Scott, 104, 137
"Social Change and the Meaning of the American Revolution" (Lockridge), 137, 138, 150
Social concentration, 5, 62–71, 72, 83, 115, 148–152
see also Population concentration
Social diversification, 44
Social mobility, 44, 59–60, 69, 72, 83, 141, 151–152
Social status, 31–32, 87
association with literacy, 6, 72, 73, 83–85, 97, 154, 156
disassociation of literacy with, 21–27, 32, 42, 114, 135–137
Solomon, L., 144
"Some Social Psychological Effects and Non-Effects of Literacy in a New Nation" (Inkeles, Schuman, and Smith), 137
Sources of literacy, 43–71, 124–125, 126, 141–152
in ideal study, 112–114
public schools, 4, 50–51, 57–59, 60, 62–71, 75, 77–78, 99, 115, 117–118, 144, 146–147
Puritan education tradition, 6, 43, 44–45, 46, 48, 49–51, 58, 64, 69, 72, 73, 74, 86, 97–101, 105, 141, 142, 143, 151, 157
social concentration 5, 62–71, 72, 83, 115, 148–152
traditional forces, 43, 49, 52–57, 143–146
transmission by migrants, 5, 10, 44–48, 49, 50, 51–52, 74–75, 78–79, 112–113, 115, 126, 136, 153, 154

[163]

AUG 1 1 1978

134437

LIBRARY OF MOUNT ST. MARY'S COLLEGE